THE OBSERVER'S BOOK OF
CACTI
AND OTHER SUCCULENTS

The Observer's Books

THE OBSERVER'S BOOK OF

CACTI

AND OTHER SUCCULENTS

By

S. H. SCOTT

HON. SEC., NATIONAL CACTUS AND SUCCULENT SOCIETY

*Describing over 300 species, with
16 plates in full colour and 66 photographs
in black and white*

FREDERICK WARNE & CO. LTD.
LONDON

FREDERICK WARNE & CO. INC.
NEW YORK

PRINTED IN GREAT BRITAIN

CONTENTS

LIST OF ILLUSTRATIONS

7

PREFACE

WITHIN recent years, more and more people have become interested in the collecting and growing of succulent plants. Botanists and plant enthusiasts at home and in other countries have long realized their fascination, and have devoted much time to the study of these plants and to methods of cultivation. So with the growth of knowledge and understanding has come increasing appreciation among people in all walks of life of their wonder, and even beauty. Beauty, they say, is in the eye of the beholder, and surely, you think, this must be a case in point. But no! Succulent plants possess in full measure that beauty which man is only now beginning to discover for himself—functional beauty. Succulent plants have adapted themselves perfectly to the conditions under which they have been forced to grow and develop, and their beauty is much more than skin deep.

There is in most of us the urge to collect. From the assiduous autograph hunter to the collector of orchids, the itch is there, only conditioned by circumstances of means and opportunity. Many of us prefer living to inanimate objects for our collections, so that we may have the further interest of watching the changes and developments which take place; but today, when time to look after a collection and available space in which to house it are in short supply, this preference cannot always be indulged. These, perhaps, may be two of the reasons why so many people have become interested in the cultivation of cacti and other succulent plants, for these plants can be left for periods without attention and those without greenhouse accommodation can enjoy growing them in the home on window-ledges.

Because these plants have developed adaptations for overcoming periods of drought, they require much less attention than do other plants. If they fall victims to a certain amount of neglect, due to the hectic conditions of modern life, they do not immediately sicken and die, for in their natural environment they are used to a great deal of hardship at the hands of nature.

The lack of knowledge of the needs of succulent plants has in the past been the cause of much misunderstanding and disappointment. This ignorance probably gave rise to the belief that cacti do not flower, or that they seldom do so. The truth is that many bear lovely and delicate flowers with a texture of petal and colouring unique in the plant world, and with right treatment will produce flowers regularly.

The operative words in the last sentence are "right treatment". This is fundamentally simple, but it must be studied. It is for the purpose of attempting to explain this treatment that the book has been undertaken, as well as to provide the reader with information which will help in the identification of succulent plants.

The author is grateful to Mr. F. W. Bartram, Nottingham, for undertaking the preparation of the line drawings which help to illustrate items in the text, and also to the National Cactus & Succulent Society for the use of several photographs.

Finally, no claim is made for completeness in the subject matter of the text, which must obviously be strictly limited if the book is not to become unwieldy.

S. H. SCOTT

INTRODUCTION

SUCCULENT plants are found widely distributed throughout the world. They are essentially distinguished from other plants because of their whole habit, their characteristic form, and their diversity of shape and colour.

Most of these plants are found in regions where there is slight rainfall, dry air, much sunshine, porous soils, and high temperature during part of the year, and these conditions have given rise to modifications of plant structures, resulting in greatly increased thickening of the stems, the leaves and sometimes the roots, enabling them to store moisture from the infrequent rains and protect themselves against excessive evaporation.

For centuries they have struggled for existence in antagonistic surroundings, and have developed into a race of independent plants, having conquered the difficulties of living.

To cultivate succulent plants successfully, every endeavour should be made to imitate as nearly as possible the conditions prevailing in their native habitats, and this is reasonably possible when they are cultivated in living-rooms and greenhouses, where watering can be controlled and warm dry air congenial to their growth can be provided.

Because most succulent plants are children of the sun, it is necessary for success with them to give them all the sunshine possible. In this country, it is true, we lack sunshine of the strength and amount they are used to, but if the plants are given a light position in the greenhouse or on the window-sill, they respond to what sunshine they get.

All succulent plants require a period of rest during which moisture is withheld. This period varies with the type of plant; some of them rest from October to March and others from December to August. These resting periods may seem difficult for the beginner to understand, and so make it hard to know when to water the plants, but the information given in this book will help to overcome this difficulty.

WHAT ARE CACTUS AND OTHER SUCCULENT PLANTS?

It is a remarkable fact that there is probably no family of plants which as a whole has aroused the interest and curiosity of plant lovers to such a degree as cacti. Nearly everyone is familiar with at least one kind of cactus, but to distinguish between members of the cactus family and the many other succulent plants requires a little knowledge. Cacti (Fig. 1) form a separate family of succulent plants characterized by the fact that, with few exceptions, they bear no leaves, or only very small, insignificant ones. They have, however, developed highly distended, juicy green stems, frequently of strange shapes, which, besides fulfilling the general purpose of serving as ducts or reservoirs for the storage of water and nourishment, also carry out the physiological processes of the missing leaves; besides this they are mostly heavily armed with spines and glochids, or barbed hairs. The spines grow from areoles which look like miniature pincushions. The aeroles are the

ECHINOCEREUS

ECHINOCACTUS

OPUNTIA

RHIPSALIS

TYPES OF CACTI

FIG. I

15

ALOE

PACHYPHYTUM

ECHEVERIA

STAPELIA

CONOPHYTUM

FENESTRARIA

DIVERSITY OF SHAPE AND FORM IN SUCCULENT PLANTS

FIG. 2

hall-mark of all cacti. All plants belonging to the cactus family have five characteristics in common (Fig. 3).

(*a*) Each seed has two cotyledons. This means that the seed is composed of two halves, like a bean. When the seed germinates, these halves, which are seed leaves, appear at the same time.

(*b*) The fruit is a berry enclosing the seeds; the berry is one-celled, having no divisions or partitions to divide it into sections as in an orange.

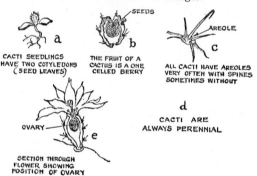

CACTI SEEDLINGS
HAVE TWO COTYLEDONS
(SEED LEAVES)

THE FRUIT OF A
CACTUS IS A ONE
CELLED BERRY

ALL CACTI HAVE AREOLES
VERY OFTEN WITH SPINES
SOMETIMES WITHOUT

CACTI ARE
ALWAYS PERENNIAL

SECTION THROUGH
FLOWER SHOWING
POSITION OF OVARY

THE FIVE FACTORS DENOTING A CACTUS

FIG. 3

(*c*) Areoles, or spine-cushions, are always present. In some kinds of cacti, the spines are absent, but the cushions are usually armed with spines or with fine hairs that are barbed at the ends (glochids) or with both spines and glochids (Fig. 4).

(*d*) All plants of the cactus family live year after year, and for this reason are said to be perennial.

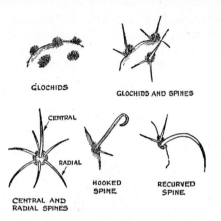

GLOCHIDS

GLOCHIDS AND SPINES

CENTRAL

RADIAL

CENTRAL AND
RADIAL SPINES

HOOKED
SPINE

RECURVED
SPINE

GLOCHIDS AND SPINES

FIG. 4

(*e*) The petals of the flower always arise from the top of the fruit or ovary.

Many plants have some of the five characteristics, but they must have all of them to belong to the family of cacti.

Plant life is divided into many different families, and one of these, the Cactaceae family, includes all cactus plants. There are, however, many other plant families which include plants that can be described as succulent but are not cacti, and collectively these are referred to as "The Other Succulents" (Fig. 2). Hence the term, "Cactus and Other Succulent Plants".

The other succulents are so intimately associated with cacti, that it is essential to have a clear understanding as to what kind of plants make up this group.

Plate 1. Collection of cacti
Cleistocactus Strausii, Notocactus Graessneri
Astrophytum asterias

Plate 2. An indoor collection of succulent plants

This group of plants may be divided into leaf and stem succulents; that is, species with thick and juicy leaves, or with excessively thick and fleshy stems and branches; there are also species with fleshy leaves and stems.

Many of these succulents are veritable plant gems, so intricate in form, delicate in colour, and beautiful when in flower, that they cannot fail to arouse our admiration. The most remarkable forms are probably to be found amongst the Mesembryanthemums (Fig. 5), which have in recent years attracted so much attention by their protective adaptation in form and colour to their environment, a phenomenon known as "mimicry".

A very large number of succulent plants are endemic to Africa, but they are to be found in all countries of the world, wherever vegetation from any cause whatsoever experiences difficulty in obtaining its water supply. They occur in the arid deserts, on high mountains, or in cold regions where the absorption of water is rendered difficult owing to intense cold, amongst rocks and sand through which rain-water drains quickly, or in brackish areas where salt impedes the absorption of water by the plants.

These conditions have given rise to very great modifications of plant structures and functions, enabling the plants to store and conserve water, to reduce loss of water from transpiration, and to increase rapid absorption by the roots.

The plants are diverse in form, and grow in almost any conceivable shape. Some are as large as trees, and some the size of a button, but all are fascinating.

CONOPHYTUM

PLEIOSPILOS

TITANOPSIS

MITROPHYLLUM

LITHOPS

LAPIDARIA

FAUCARIA

CONOPHYTUM

MESEMBRYANTHEMUMS

FIG. 5

20

HOW TO START A COLLECTION

Succulents are accommodating plants; and they are much less exacting with regard to housing and treatment than many other plants.

In starting a collection, much depends on the attitude of mind of the person proposing to start it— whether it is desired to grow a few plants only, or a representative collection. Whichever decision is made, the essential point is to deal successfully with them, and not merely to possess them, for their cultivation differs somewhat from the treatment usually afforded to other plants.

The first step is to decide where you are going to keep the plants. They may be grown in a green-house, where heating is available in winter; or in a cold frame during summer, and transferred to a living-room for the winter; or the frame can be heated, and the plants kept in it permanently; or the collection can be accommodated all the year round in a really sunny south window, where in summer air and light can reach them, but which is open as little as possible in winter.

The next step is to secure some of the more easily grown plants to begin with. There is a temptation in the first heat of enthusiasm to try to acquire as many different kinds of succulents as possible in the least possible time. It is best, however, to acquire a few, care for these, gain a little experience, and gradually add to the collection.

GENERAL CULTIVATION

The successful cultivation of succulent plants is dependent on soil, temperature, light, and moisture.

The compost in which to grow succulent plants must be of open texture and suitable consistency. One containing 2 parts loam, 1 part leaf-mould or peat, and 1 part sharp sand, with the addition of a small quantity of old mortar rubble (obtained from old buildings) to provide lime, and a few pieces of charcoal to help to keep the compost sweet, is very suitable for most kinds, but where special mixtures of compost are preferable this has been indicated in the text.

Enthusiasts vary these proportions and ingredients to suit specific purposes. Should you not wish to mix your own, suitable composts for cacti and other succulent plants are usually obtainable from seedsmen, and of these the John Innes Compost No. 1, with an addition of sharp sand (5 parts compost to 1 part sand) has been found to give excellent results for most succulents. For the more vigorous growers such as Opuntias, Cerei, Crassulas, Sedums, etc., John Innes Compost No. 2, with sand in the same proportion, is to be preferred.

It must be pointed out, however, that a few cacti, such as Epiphyllums or Rhipsalis, require a more nutritious diet, and for these plants a compost consisting of 2 parts leaf-mould, 1 part loam, and 1 part sharp sand is recommended. One thing they do not like is lime in any form, so this should be withheld.

TEMPERATURE

From about the middle of May, the temperature is such that cactus and other succulent plants may be grown out of doors, but about the end of September the plants must be brought indoors, for soon

Plate 3. Cristate cacti. P.36
Succulent plants used in formal bedding

Plate 4. *Opuntia tunicata.* P.44

the temperature, especially at night, begins to fall. Succulent plants require protection from frost. The best winter temperature for greenhouse or window collections is around 45°F., but if the temperature now and then drops a few degrees at night, it will not harm the plants. In the home, where fires or central heating are in use, rooms can become very warm, and the air very dry; these conditions are not relished by most plants, but succulents are scarcely affected, another proof that they are the most suitable plants for modern dwellings. This warm atmosphere in winter, however, tends to keep succulent plants growing instead of entering, as they should do, upon their winter's rest which is necessary for the production of their flowers the following season. In such conditions, therefore, it is wise to bear this in mind and keep them in a cool position.

LIGHT AND AIR

Whilst most cacti and other succulents require plenty of light and sunshine, some prefer shade or half shade. Rhipsalis, Epiphyllums and their relations thrive best in shade with only about two hours' sunshine late on a sunny afternoon.

Seedlings also should have some shade from strong sunshine, especially during the hotter hours, for they are yet tender and too much sunshine may disfigure the plants through burning.

Other plants, such as Crassulas, Haworthias, Gasterias, or Ceropegias prefer half shade. All succulents need plenty of fresh air.

Frames, greenhouses, etc., should be well ventilated at all times whenever weather conditions permit.

After their enforced winter's rest, most succulents usually start their new growth in March, when watering should commence. To begin with only small quantities of water should be given, for the plants are not fully active yet. During April and May they might require watering once a week, and throughout the summer more frequently; if the weather is sunny and hot the plants may need watering every day.

It is always best to give a thorough watering, and then allow the compost to become nearly dry before watering again.

Beginners may be perplexed when water takes a long time to penetrate the surface of the compost. This may be due to faulty drainage in the pot, or to excessive dryness of the soil.

If the former is the cause, the plant should be repotted; if the latter, then stand the pot immersed to just under the rim in a container of water, until the compost is thoroughly wetted.

About the end of September, water should be gradually withheld in order to prepare the plants for their winter's rest. The plants have to harden their tissues, and become more or less inactive. If they are kept active by frequent watering, they are in no condition to withstand low temperatures and winter humidity.

During winter, the plants should be kept almost dry, in a cool and airy place; but in order to prevent the roots from drying up completely, a little water may be necessary about once a month. Excess water and warmth, if given, will start a winter growth, and may result in few flowers being produced the following spring.

It must be pointed out, however, that some succulent plants differ with regard to their resting periods. This is because habitat seasons vary. For instance, in South Africa, in the broad coastal area on the western and southern regions, the rainy period is from April to September, and in the interior region from October to March; these rainy seasons are the growing and flowering periods of plants endemic to these areas.

It is, however, easy when growing plants indoors to imitate these conditions as found in nature by withholding or giving moisture in accordance with the dormant or growing periods.

If rain-water is available, it is best for the plants; otherwise use tap water.

SEED RAISING

Impatience is an almost universal trait of character, and cactus growers are not altogether immune from this malady. We demand mature plants for our collections, but we are missing a lot of pleasure if, by impatience, we overlook the fascinating pastime of raising succulents from seed. The essentials for successful cultivation are few and simple. Many people have been disappointed and discouraged in their first attempts to grow seedlings and feel it is a somewhat complicated process. This is not true. The growing of these plants from seed is so simple that anyone with normal intelligence may easily succeed.

The information about to be given will not be sufficient to cope with every emergency, but it will make possible sufficient initial success to encourage the reader to go on with this delightful and interesting hobby.

The seeds of some succulents will germinate as soon after maturity as they are placed in favourable conditions, whilst the seeds of others cannot be coaxed to grow before the following season. Of course, this does not apply only to the seeds of succulent plants, but to many other plants also.

To raise plants satisfactorily from seed it is necessary to provide a suitable temperature and compost and moisture, and once the little plants are showing, light and air are essential.

Since succulents are for the most part tropical or sub-tropical plants, it is to be expected that the seed will germinate best at relatively high temperatures. The ideal is a uniform temperature of about 80°F. The method used to secure this uniform heat depends much on the means available, and the ingenuity of the grower. Simple apparatus can be easily made in the form of a box with a glass cover, with an electric bulb so arranged under the seed pan that it will give sufficient additional heat. More elaborate propagators can be purchased from firms who manufacture them, and many of these excellent propagators are thermostatically controlled and are ideal for germination of seeds and the raising of seedlings.

Not everyone, however, can provide even an improvised propagator, but this need· not deter anyone from attempting to raise seedlings, for alternate arrangements can be made to utilize such warm parts of the home as a hot airing-cupboard, or perhaps a place can be found on top of a radiator, etc.; and finally, if it is not possible to provide heat, delay sowing the seeds until May, for by then the weather is warmer and congenial for growth. If one

Plate 5. *Opuntia verschaffeltii.* P.45

Plate 6. *Opuntia leptocaulis.* P. 45   *Opuntia polyantha.* P. 46

can provide the necessary heat, the seeds should be sown early in the year, in late January or February, to obtain the maximum growth before the next winter.

There is much difference of opinion as to the best compost to use in the seed pans or pots, but it is generally recognized that John Innes Compost No. 1 with some sharp sand added will produce very satisfactory results. Sterilized John Innes composts are obtainable from seedsmen.

To prepare the seed receptacles, first make sure they are thoroughly clean. Indeed, if new or sterilized pots or pans are used, so much the better, for, in addition to using sterilized compost, the risk of your seedlings damping off is greatly reduced. Some coarse material such as crocks should be placed in the bottom of the containers to ensure the necessary drainage. Cover this with a fine layer of peat and then fill up the container to within half an inch of the top with the compost. As the pot is filled, tap it on the table to consolidate the compost. The fine layer of peat is provided to prevent the drainage becoming blocked. Sprinkle a little coarse sand on the surface and sow the seeds thinly and as evenly as possible on the top. Small seeds should not be covered, as any resistance offered to the germinating seed may cause it to fail. Larger seed should, however, be covered to a depth of not more than the thickness of the seed.

Water may now be applied by gently sprinkling or spraying the surface until all the compost is thoroughly damp, or the container may be set in another dish of water until capillary attraction has brought moisture to the top. Although it is a little more trouble, the latter method is to be preferred.

Top water is apt to cause the soil to "puddle" and seal the surface so as to exclude air which is as vital to the young plants as is water.

Cover each container with a small glass sheet, as this ensures quick germination. Moisture will sometimes accumulate on the under side of the glass, and if it falls it may injure the seedlings or wash the compost from above the seeds. It is therefore a good practice to remove the moisture once or twice a day.

As soon as a reasonable number of seedlings appear, remove the glass from the container and allow more air to reach the plants. The surface of the compost should be kept moist at all times. Any neglect that permits the newly germinated seeds to become dry, even for a short time, is fatal to them.

The seed containers should not be placed in direct sunshine because the young plants cannot withstand the strong light. The containers may be kept in the shade or the glass may be covered with paper to ensure shade.

Admit some air when the seeds germinate, but continue to provide shade. If growth is rapid it may be necessary to prick out the seedlings in the first season, but generally they appear to do better if left undisturbed until the following spring.

POTTING AND REPOTTING

Before a plant is placed in a pot, the roots should be examined carefully. All roots that show any indication of being rotted should be cut back to clean, healthy tissue, and any dead roots cut off. If all the roots are in bad condition, then cut them all off, and re-root afresh, to ensure that the plant is free from diseased tissue.

Select a pot just a little wider than the plant body, which will comfortably accommodate the roots; for instance, use a three-inch pot or pan for a plant that is two inches in diameter. Allowance, however, must be made for the height and general size of those plants which grow taller.

Use a clean pot and place a piece of crock arch-wise over the drainage hole, so that there is a hollow space over the hole, then place sufficient smaller crocks, about a quarter of the depth of the pot, to ensure good drainage, and then a little of the compost on top. The plant is held in one hand, and the soil is filled in with the other and pressed firmly around the plant. To ensure proper distribution of the compost between the roots, the pot and plant should be tapped lightly on the table. To leave room for watering, the pot is not filled to the rim but to within half an inch or so. Newly potted plants should not be immediately watered, but only after a few days, for moisture might easily cause decay in broken or damaged roots.

Repotting is an operation governed by the same principles as those followed in original plantings.

Some enthusiasts repot both small and large plants annually, but this is not normally necessary. As long as a plant appears vigorous and healthy, it is best left undisturbed, except perhaps young plants in small pots which require a change of compost and, of course, any plants that have become too large for their pots.

Large specimens are repotted every two or three years.

The best time to repot is in the spring, as soon as the plants show new growth.

PROPAGATION FROM CUTTINGS
AND OFFSETS

CUTTINGS

Sizeable cuttings should be selected. This will ensure quicker flowering specimens. They are taken during the plant's period of growth from April to August. When taking a cutting, use a sharp knife or razor blade so that a clean cut can be made. The cut surfaces should be dusted with flowers of sulphur and left for two or three days in the sun (or longer depending on the species) in order that the cut surface may harden and form a callus. This will prevent decay. The cuttings should be placed in very sandy compost, consisting of 3 parts sand and 1 part sifted loam, with the base of each cutting just penetrating the surface soil; if possible, cover them with a piece of glass in order to obtain quicker rooting. Until rooting does take place, water should be given sparingly, and afterwards somewhat more generously.

Epiphyllums, Rhipsalis, and Euphorbias root well in a compost of equal parts of fine sand and sifted peat.

When the cuttings have formed roots, they can be transplanted into a mixture of 2 parts loam, 1 part leaf-mould or peat, and 1 part sand, with a sprinkling of bone meal added to each pot, as well as a little mortar rubble or lime.

OFFSETS

Offsets are complete plants developed on the parent plant. Often roots are formed on them before they are detached. They are easily separated

Plate 7. *Opuntia diademata.* P.47

Plate 8. Flowers of *Opuntia versicolor* (variable in colour). P.47

from the parent and, if rooted, should be potted up at once and given a light watering and treated like ordinary plants. If no roots are attached, treat them as cuttings.

Unlike seedlings, which might be variable, cuttings and offsets are always true to type. Many cactus genera produce offsets freely, particularly Echinopsis, Mammillarias, Lobivias, and Rebutias.

PROPAGATION FROM LEAF CUTTINGS

Most Echeverias, Pachyphytums, Sedums, and Crassulas can be propagated from leaf cuttings. Detach a few single leaves from the stem by exerting sideways pressure on the leaves, so that they come off cleanly. Place these in dry sand and keep in partial shade. Soon small plants will appear, which can be potted. Leave the old leaf attached to the young plant until it is well established and growing.

GRAFTING

Grafting is another method of propagating plants. It consists of uniting a piece of one plant called the *scion*, with another rooted plant called the *stock*. The tissues of the two parts make union and the scion continues to grow while the stock provides the food for the growth.

Grafting is resorted to for a variety of purposes, such as accelerating growth of slow-growing plants, preserving species that do not grow well on their own roots in cultivation, obtaining a greater number of flowers, developing bushy and more decorative plants, or preserving abnormal forms such as crests and monstrous plants.

Cacti are frequently grafted. The best time for the

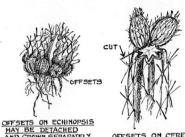

OFFSETS ON ECHINOPSIS
MAY BE DETACHED
AND GROWN SEPARATELY

OFFSETS ON CEREUS
MAY BE CUT OFF
WHERE SHOWN

WHERE TO CUT PAD
ON OPUNTIA

PLANTLET ON
PACHYPHYTUM LEAF

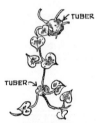

SHOOT OF ZYGOCACTUS
SHOWING
AERIAL ROOTS

SHOOT OF CEROPEGIA
SHOWING AERIAL TUBERS
WHICH MAY BE
PLANTED SEPARATELY

PROPAGATION

FIG. 6

Plate 9. *Opuntia subulata*. P.47

Plate 10. *Opuntia erinacea*. P.48

operation is from May to September when the plants are growing well. It is very important that both the scion and the stock should be in vigorous growing condition. Many grafts do not take properly due to the violation of this requirement.

There are three kinds of grafts commonly employed—the cleft, the flat, and the side.

The cleft graft is very simple, and easily made. The stock is cut off to the height at which it is desired to have the new plant develop. A long V-shaped notch is cut in the top of the stock. The cut should never be longer than the insert if a perfect union is to be attained. The stem of the scion is then cut on two sides to form a wedge, and inserted into the split of the stock. The cut faces should be perfectly flat planes and not curved or irregular surfaces. In order to keep the scion from slipping out of place, it is necessary to fasten it securely. This can be done conveniently by pinning it with one or two long cactus spines. The spines are thrust into the stock so that they pass through the wedge of the scion, and in order to keep the sides of the notch from spreading it is good practice to wrap some string or raffia around the graft. The string should be taut enough to hold the scion in place, and yet not so tight as to cut into it, or the stock. Much of the success will be measured by the skill in cutting the stock and scion to a perfect fit.

In the flat graft, both scion and stock should be of approximately the same width at the intended union. After selecting the two plants, make a smooth transverse cut on each specimen and then place the scion on the severed stock, pressing the two flat surfaces together. To hold the scion in place, use two large rubber bands, placing them gently over the top of the scion, and running them underneath the flower-pot. String can also be used, but first file four small grooves on the rim and bottom of the flower-pot to prevent the string from slipping.

The side graft requires no special operation beyond slicing one side of both scion and stock and fixing the two joints in place.

When grafting operations are completed, place the plants in a warm but shaded place so that the cut surfaces will not dry out too rapidly. The stock plant should be watered in the normal way, but take care that no moisture reaches the graft. Inspection should be made occasionally to note whether the union has properly formed.

PESTS AND THEIR CONTROL

Succulent plants grown in the home and green-house are liable to attacks from a few common garden pests, chiefly aphids, mealy bugs, scale insects, thrips, red spiders, and root mealy bugs.

Aphids are either black, green or yellow, soft-bodied insects. A nicotine spray or any of the recommended insecticides obtainable from seeds-men will easily control them.

Mealy Bugs are recognized because they cover themselves with a white cotton substance. They should never be allowed a foothold on plants, for they breed and spread rapidly. A petroleum emulsion is effective, or methylated spirits with $2\frac{1}{2}$ per cent nicotine added (20 drops of nicotine to an ounce of spirit), and applied with a camel-hair brush, will quickly destroy them.

Scale Insects are tiny creatures with a protective shell-like covering. They fasten themselves to stems, branches and leaves, where they extract the juices. In advanced stages they completely cover the stems and leaves; in such cases the plant should be placed on its side, and the scales brushed off with a stiff tooth-brush or similar brush, or an oil emulsion spray is effective in smothering them.

Thrips are quick-moving brown or black insects which look like animated grains of pepper. They rasp the tissues of plants and can do considerable damage. An insecticide containing nicotine will control them.

Red Spiders thrive under hot and dry conditions and multiply very rapidly. They are very small yellowish to reddish insects and can cause much damage to plants. Spraying the plants frequently with water will discourage these pests. In a greenhouse, the most effective way to destroy them is by fumigation. For this purpose azobenzene cones are to be recommended. Dusting with derris dust is also effective. This should be applied three times at intervals of three days. Spraying with DDT is also effective.

Root Mealy Bugs attack the roots of plants. The pests are plainly visible as white patches adhering to the roots, and on the inside of the pot. They are effectively dealt with by immersing the potted plant in warm water containing a strong nicotine solution (one teaspoonful of pure nicotine to a quart of water) and allowing it to remain there for twenty or thirty minutes, or by removing the plant from the pot, shaking the soil off the roots and dipping it in methylated spirits to which has been added pure nicotine (one teaspoonful of nicotine to a quart of spirits). Most of the attacks are spread by ants.

CRISTATE AND MONSTROUS FORMS

Malformations may occur in all species of plants Little is known of the origin of such abnormalities The phenomenon is referred to as fasciation.

The terminal or growing centre of a plant is composed of rapidly multiplying cells which constitute the meristem. In rare instances, a plant will develop meristems at a number of points on one stem, producing the phenomenon known as a monstrous form.

In other rare instances, the meristem widens into a line rather than a point, and this form is known as a cristate form or crest.

Insect damage to the growing centre may be one cause. Recent experiments have also proved that radio-active soil usually causes fasciation.

Another phenomenon is that a monstrous or cristate plant may suddenly again produce normal branches and shoots.

Such plants as *Opuntia clavarioides cristata*, *Opuntia cylindrica cristata*, *Cereus Peruvianus monstrosus*, *Echinopsis tubiflora cristata*, and *Rebutia minuscula cristata* are often seen in collections.

BOWL GARDENS

If you desire an interesting and fascinating diversion, plant a bowl garden with succulent plants. When you build such a garden, you may be sure that no one else has one just like it, for it provides you with an opportunity to express your artistic taste.

It is possible to achieve so many different lay-outs that it is neither practical nor desirable to give in detail possible arrangements. It is much better to indicate those general principles which must be followed to ensure success, and leave all the details of obtaining the artistic effect to the creative imagination of the individual.

A harmonious arrangement of plants and rocks can have an artistic appeal and give satisfaction and pleasure to the owner.

The containers may be bowls of any shape and size, with or without drainage hole, glazed or porous, and should be at least 3 inches to $3\frac{1}{2}$ inches deep, according to the size. This depth will allow for adequate drainage. A decorative piece of pottery adds charm and beauty to an arrangement, or you may decide to select a bowl of neutral colour. Materials for your work consist of broken crocks or brick for drainage, a suitable compost in which to grow the plants, pieces of charcoal to keep the soil from souring, sharp sand, and very small gravel or chippings to dress the top of the bowl. Miniature bridges, mirror lakes or houses may be used for scenic effects.

Place the materials on a table so that everything is handy. If the bowl has a drainage hole, cover this with a piece of broken flower-pot placed archwise over the hole, and fill to nearly half-way up with crocks, broken down to very small pieces, and a few pieces of charcoal, and add the soil mixture (see section on soil).

With the container filled, temporarily place the

plants on top so as to acquire some idea of artistic composition, then remove the plants and start planting according to your scheme of arrangement. If a few pieces of rock, such as tufa, limestone, or sandstone, are placed amongst the plants, the general effect is all the more pleasing.

It may be desired to arrange the compost and rocks so as to give the appearance of a little hillside, and in bowl gardens of this nature the general rule is to place the larger pieces of rock at the base of the incline, which will naturally bring them into the foreground. This gives the impression of a heavier and more substantial foundation.

When the plants and rocks are in position, thinly cover the soil with sand, very small gravel, or chippings. This will give the bowl garden a finished appearance.

It is wise not to water the succulent plants immediately after planting, but delay watering for a few days, in case any damage has been caused to the roots during planting.

Always keep a bowl garden in the sunniest window of the house. Light is essential for succulent plants. In poorly lighted places chlorophyll cannot be produced, and death from starvation is inevitable.

Every week, turn the bowl so as to keep the plants growing reasonably straight, as they will always tend to grow towards the light.

If a non-porous bowl without a drainage hole is used, great care must be exercised in watering. Excess water cannot get away except by evaporation through the soil, and if the plants are overwatered, excess water may be lodging in the bottom of the bowl, which in time would cause souring of the soil.

Plate 11. *Opuntia Bigelovii*. P.44

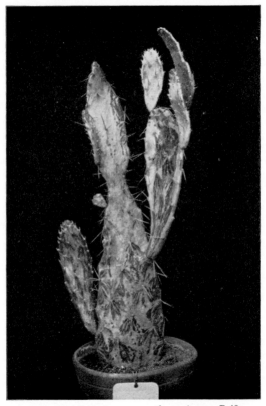

Plate 12. *Opuntia monacantha variegata.* P.49

When watering the bowl, remember to water well and allow the soil to dry out before giving more; this drying out applies not only to the top layer of soil but to the bottom layer as well. Watering will take place more frequently in hot summer weather. In winter, watering will be less frequent; at this season, if the bowl is kept in a heated room, water may be required every two or three weeks; in an unheated room, when frost is not about, once in every five to six weeks.

Many varieties of interesting succulent plants are available for use in bowl gardens, and the following may be noted:

Opuntia microdasys, O. leptocaulis, Echinocactus Grusonii (seedling), *Ferocactus Wislizenii* (seedling), *Rebutia Fiebrigii, R. minuscula, R. pygmaea, R. rubispina, R. deminuta, Mammillaria elongata, M. bombycina, M. celsiana, M. bocasana, M. pusilla, M. prolifera, Chamaecereus Silvestrii, Crassula Cooperi, C. socialis, C. tetragona, C. quadrangularis, C. pyramidalis, C. argentea, Aeonium Simsii, A. Lindleyi, A. Haworthii, Echeveria Derenbergii, E. carnicolor, E. farinosa, E. leucotricha, E. pulvinata, E. setosa, Oscularia deltoides, Delosperma echinatum, Sedum Treleasei, S. Adolphii, S. pachyphyllum, S. Stahlii, Haworthia tessellata, H. fasciata, H. margaritifera, Senecio articulata* (sometimes referred to as *Kleinia articulata*).

CLASSIFICATION OF SUCCULENT PLANTS

It is not considered necessary here to give a technical discussion of the grouping of plants. It is, however, necessary and essential for the reader to have a general understanding of the meaning of such group names as family, tribe, genus, species, and variety.

The *family* includes those plants which have in common certain characteristics which the botanists consider indicate a definite, but in some cases rather distant, relationship; for instance, the rose and the apple belong to the same family, and it may be rather a shock to learn that the potato, the tomato, and the tobacco plant are all members of the same family.

There are members of the cactus family which differ quite as widely from one another as these plants mentioned, and this equally applies to the other succulents; indeed, there are plants amongst the other succulents which look very much like cacti, and it is very easy for the beginner to mistake these for true cacti. However, with a little experience the beginner will soon be able to differentiate between the two.

The term *tribe* applies only to the family Cactaceae, which is divided into three groups known as tribes. The members of each tribe have not only the characteristics of the family but they have other characteristics which set them apart from the rest of the family. The tribes are divided

Plate 13. *Cephalocereus senilis*, the "old man" cactus. P.52

Flowers of *Trichocereus macrogonus*. P.57

Plate 14. *Trichocereus spachianus*. P.57

Plate 15. Flowers of *Harrisia Bonplandii*. P.58
Flowers of *Harrisia Martinii*. P.58

Plate 16. *Cleistocactus Strausii*. P.58

into smaller groups, each known as a *genus* (plural *genera*).

Members of a genus resemble each other much more closely than do members of the family. Each species has additional characteristics common to all other members of the genus.

The genus is composed of groups of individuals designated as *species*; that is, groups of individuals which resemble each other in all their constant characteristics.

Occasionally, a group of individuals within a species has one or more characters more or less persistent, but not important enough to warrant its consideration as a separate species. These individuals are known as *varieties*.

The classification of the other succulents is by family, sub-family, genus, species, and variety.

CACTI

CLASSIFICATION OF THE CACTACEAE

TRIBE I
PEIRESKIEAE

Peireskia

TRIBE II
OPUNTIEAE

Opuntia
Nopalea, etc.

TRIBE III. CEREEAE

Sub-Tribe I. CEREANAE

Cereus
Monvillea
Cephalocereus
Espostoa
Oreocereus
Pachycereus
Lemaireocereus
Wilcoxia
Nyctocereus
Heliocereus
Trichocereus
Harrisia
Cleistocactus
Carnegiea
Lophocereus, etc.

Sub-Tribe II
HYLOCEREANAE

Hylocereus
Selenicereus
Aporocactus, etc.

Sub-Tribe III
ECHINOCEREANAE

Echinocereus
Chamaecereus
Rebutia
Lobivia
Mediolobivia
Echinopsis, etc.

Sub-Tribe IV
ECHINOCACTANAE

Ariocarpus
Obregonia
Lophophora
Aztekium
Epithelantha
Hamatocactus
Leuchtenbergia
Stenocactus
Ferocactus
Echinomastus
Gymnocalycium
Echinocactus
Astrophytum
Notocactus
Parodia, etc.

Sub-Tribe V. CACTANAE

Discocactus
Cactus

Sub-Tribe VI
CORYPHANTHANAE

Thelocactus
Coryphantha
Mammillaria
Dolichothele, etc.

Sub-Tribe VII
EPIPHYLLANAE

Zygocactus
Schlumbergera
Epiphyllum, etc.

Sub-Tribe VIII
RHIPSALIDANAE

Erythrorhipsalis
Rhipsalis, etc.

Plate 17. Flower of *Selenicereus pteranthus*, Queen of the Night. P.61

Plate 18. *Opuntia spinosior* flowering in the desert. P. 44

Tribe I. PEIRESKIEAE

PEIRESKIA. These plants are natives of tropical America. A few are ornamental and desirable plants. They have the appearance of ordinary shrubs, and bear little resemblance to cacti at all. Their stems are not fleshy but are strong woody trunks with ordinary green though somewhat thick rubber-like leaves. They must be looked upon as a primeval form of cacti, and may constitute the link between the cacti of today and their ancestral forms.

Peireskia aculeata. A climbing shrub. Areoles have 1 to 3 short hooked spines. Leaves long, elliptical, pointed and short-stalked, with a prominent mid-rib. Flowers whitish and strongly perfumed. This plant is often used as stock for grafting *Zygocactus truncatus*.

Peireskia godseffiana. This plant has beautifully coloured leaves, red, apricot-yellow, and green on the upper side, and reddish-purple on the under side.

Peireskia grandifolia. This plant bears rose-red flowers, and is perhaps the best species for cultivation.

Tribe II. OPUNTIEAE

OPUNTIA. The genus is a large one and includes both small and large types. The stems are jointed and the joints may be flat, cylindrical, clavate, or globose, bearing areoles and glochids. Many of the Opuntias have rudimentary leaves on the new growth, but these disappear with increasing age. Opuntias are not difficult plants to grow and should be potted in a mixture of 3 parts loam, 2 parts silver sand, and 1 part leaf-mould, to which is added 2 parts broken brick and a half part old mortar rubble.

Opuntia salmiana. S. Brazil, Paraguay, and N.

America. One of the few Opuntias which will flower fairly readily in our collections. Areoles small, but have many glochids and 3 to 5 yellowish spines. Flowers, numerous, yellowish passing to reddish.

Opuntia cylindrica. Ecuador and Peru. An easy species to grow. Joints cylindrical, and the young growth produces cylindrical leaves which soon drop off. Areoles whitish, and spines whitish, 2 to 3 in number. Flowers, red. A cristate form is also in cultivation.

Opuntia vestita. Bolivia. Stems erect or sprawling; rudimentary leaves persisting for some time; areoles round, yellowish, with long white glochids; spines number 4 to 8. Associated with many long, white hairs, which almost entirely cover the stem. Prefers half shade. Some beautiful cristate forms are in cultivation.

Opuntia floccosa. Peru and Bolivia. Stems sprawling, and coloured grass-green. Areoles large, with 1 to 3 yellow spines, which are straight and slender, and many pure white woolly curly hairs, which cover the plant. Flowers, yellow. This plant requires all the sunshine possible. A cristate form is also in cultivation.

Opuntia tunicata (Plate 4). Central Mexico, Ecuador and N. Chile. A sun-loving species, one of the most interesting of the cylindrical Opuntias, very spiny. Spines reddish and concealed in thin white papery sheaths; flowers, yellow.

Opuntia Bigelovii (Plate 11). Cylindrical joints thick; areoles round, white, with yellow glochids; spines numerous with 6 to 10 radials and 6 to 10 centrals; flowers purplish.

Opuntia spinosior (Plate 18). N. Mexico, New

Mexico and Arizona. Joints dark green, warty; spines numerous, 8 to 12, and increasing in number up to 30 as growth matures; flowers variable, white, yellow, reddish, or purple.

Opuntia fulgida. Mexico and Arizona. Areoles small, with yellowish or white glochids; spines 10 or more, sheathed; flowers, pink.

Opuntia clavarioides. Chile. A low-growing plant with joints greyish-brown, cylindrical or conical; areoles small and closely set, with 4 to 10 short white hair-like spines. A plant that rarely flowers. Usually grown as a graft on other **species** of *Opuntia*.

Opuntia verschaffeltii (Plate 5). Bolivia. Stem and joints cylindrical with leaves which persist for a long time. The flowers are beautiful, deep red and orange; the areoles whitish with yellow glochids and 1 to 3 white slender flexible spines. The plant is a slow grower and is often found in collections.

Opuntia ramosissima. Mexico, California, Nevada and Arizona. Joints slender, grey, and widely spreading. The thin-looking stems often branch on top in the shape of a cross. The areoles are often spineless, but more usually have 1 spine to each. Flowers, greenish-yellow. In its native habitat it grows on dry hillsides. There is also a pretty cristate form in cultivation.

Opuntia leptocaulis (Plate 6). Mexico, Texas and Arizona. An interesting plant for the beginner. The glochids are abundant and there are 1 to 2 brown spines in a reddish-yellow sheath. There are numerous varieties of this plant. Var. *brevispina* is free flowering.

Opuntia Kleinae. Mexico and Texas. Areoles white, glochids yellowish passing to brown, with usually only 1 spine on each areole, but sometimes 2 to 4 smaller ones are to be found. Flowers, pale pink, brownish outside.

Opuntia microdasys. N. Mexico. Erect, bushy, with oval flattened joints. The areoles are conspicuous with a prominent rounded large tuft of yellow glochids, and sometimes one short yellow spine. This plant seldom flowers in cultivation, but it is most attractive and should be included in all collections. There are a few varieties, all of which are interesting, particularly var. *albispina* which fortunately is easy to grow and very beautiful. The joints in this plant are rather small and the areoles and glochids are silvery-white. Var. *pallida* has larger joints with pale yellow areoles and glochids.

Opuntia rufida. N. Mexico and Texas. A very desirable plant with joints of a dark greyish-green, elongated, and slightly thicker than *O. microdasys*. The areoles are large, the glochids chocolate-brown; the spines are absent. It is a plant that grows well in cultivation.

Opuntia azurea. The joints are large and round, bluish-grey. The yellowish areoles bear brown or yellowish spines.

Opuntia polyantha (Plate 6). West Indies. A much-branched low bush. The joints are yellowish-green, with white areoles bearing numerous glochids and 5 to 8 yellowish-brown spines. Flowers, pale yellow.

Opuntia elata (Plate 23). Paraguay. A tall, erect plant, with elongated green joints. The areoles are well separated, large, with whitish wool. Spines are absent on the young joints; flowers, orange-yellow.

Opuntia santa-rita. Texas, California, and Arizona. This plant is quite spineless with large reddish-brown areoles, tufted with brown glochids. The joints are a rather bluish green. A very beautiful species, well worthy of cultivation.

Opuntia versicolor (Plate 26). Mexico and Arizona. A beautiful species, the flowers of which are very variable, from greenish-yellow, reddish to brown; there are 5 to 12 spines, sheathed.

Opuntia Scheerii. Mexico. Very attractive low, greyish-green plants with large oval joints. The areoles and glochids are yellowish-brown. Spines number 8 to 12 and are slender, golden yellow, with many pale yellow hairs. Flower, sulphur yellow.

Opuntia diademata (Plate 7). Sometimes grown as *O. papyracantha*. Joints oval, thick at the base, at first brownish-green passing to greyish-green; 1 to 4 spines. Flowers, pale yellow. A most interesting species, well worth growing.

Opuntia subulata (Plate 9). Chile and Argentina. In this plant the leaves are very persistent. The glochids are few and yellowish, and there are 1 or 2 pale yellow spines which are straight and strong. The plant bears large red flowers.

Opuntia ficus-indica. Widely distributed in tropical America. In its native land it is often grown for its fruits, and for forage for animals. The joints are smooth when young, and quite smooth when fully developed. The spines are almost absent; the areoles whitish, with small yellow glochids. There are numerous varieties of this species producing fruits varying in colour from white or yellow to bright crimson.

Opuntia engelmanii. Mexico, Arizona, New Mexico and Texas. A widely spreading bush, branched from the ground, with oval, elongated or

47

roundish joints. The rather large, whitish areoles bear many brown, yellow-pointed glochids and, in the middle and upper areoles, 6 to 10 spines which are white and reddish or brownish at the base. Flower, yellow. This is a very variable species.

Opuntia bergeriana. The natural habitat of this plant is not known, but it flourishes on the Italian Riviera. It is easy to grow. The flowers are deep red with pink stamens, a white style and stigma with 6 green lobes. The areoles are greyish with yellow glochids and 2 or 3 awl-shaped spines, yellow passing to grey.

Opuntia basilaris. N. Mexico and California, to Nevada, Arizona and Utah. A beautiful and most popular species. The grey-green pads sometimes turn pinkish-purple, and are thick and fan-shaped, springing from a common base. They bear no spines, but the glochids set closely over the surface belie their soft velvety look. The flowers are a lovely pale pink or carmine.

Opuntia leucotricha. Mexico. Frequently seen in amateur collections. The plant is covered with very short, greyish, velvety hair. Joints, oval. The white areoles bear yellowish glochids, and 1 to 3 white spines, later increasing in number; along with these there are numerous hair-like flexible white spines almost entirely covering the surface of the joints. The flowers are deep yellow, with white stamens and a deep red style and stigma, with 6 green lobes.

Opuntia erinacea (Plate 10). California, Arizona, Utah and Nevada. A more or less erect bushy plant, with elongated joints which are thick, flat or almost cylindrical; deep green, with closely set small and somewhat prominent white areoles. There are few glochids, but numerous spreading, slender and

Plate 19. *Echinocereus Fendleri* with flower. P.63

Plate 20. Flowers of *Echinocereus triglochidiatus*. P.64

flexible spines. The plant is often called the "grizzly bear" because of its very shaggy appearance.

Opuntia Rafinesquei. Texas, New Mexico, Kentucky, Missouri, Kansas and Tennessee. A popular plant for the beginner. The oval, elongated joints are thin and flat; the areoles are far apart and bear brown glochids; the spines are absent or borne only on marginal areoles, when they number 1 to 3; the plant bears numerous sulphur-yellow flowers, which are reddish at the base of the petals.

Opuntia monacantha (Plate 12). S. Brazil, Uruguay, Paraguay and Argentina. Grows to almost treelike proportions, with a thick stem. Joints oval, and shining green. The areoles are far apart with 1 brown spine, or sometimes 2 or 3 spines on top joints. Flower, deep yellow, with the outer petals reddish at the base. There is a very pretty variety, *O. monacantha variegata,* which has smaller joints, beautifully marbled with white or yellow, and should be represented in all collections.

Opuntia robusta. Mexico. A strong-growing variety with the joints slightly oval, thick, and greyish-green with a fine bluish hue. The areoles are brownish, the upper ones bearing 2 to 12 thick yellow spines, brown at the base, but passing to white. Flowers yellow. In cultivation it is not rare to find that the spines have disappeared completely. A very desirable species and easy to grow.

NOPALEA. These are tall plants, almost tree-like, but bearing a few glochids. The flowers are red, differing from those of *Opuntia* in that the segments of the perianth are erect, and form a sort of a tube, the stamens protruding and always longer than the petals.

49

Nopalea coccinellifera. Tropical Mexico. This plant has ascending and spreading branches. The areoles are far apart, with numerous yellow glochids; the spines are absent or small. The flower is a lovely red with pink stamens. A very desirable beginner's plant.

Tribe III. CEREEAE

Sub-Tribe 1. CEREANAE

CEREUS. The genus *Cereus* is very large, consisting of more than 200 species. The flowers are funnel-shaped, some being elongated and very showy, and they bloom mostly in the darkness of the night. Perhaps this night blooming accounts for the softness and brilliance of the delicate colourings. The plants are trees, shrubs or climbers, growing erect or spreading out with ribbed branches. They are the tallest and largest of the Cactaceae.

Cereus chalybaeus. Argentina. Has a columnar stem which when young is a beautiful blue but with age changes to dark green. There are 5 to 6 ribs with prominent areoles, furnished with brownish wool. All the spines are straight and black, the radials numbering 7 to 9, centrals 3 to 4. A very popular species, and deservedly so.

Cereus azureus. N. Argentina and S. Brazil. The stem is erect with 6 or 7 ribs, obtuse, swollen, and slightly gibbous at the areoles. Spines number 8 to 16, and are black and awl-shaped, with 2 to 4 central spines which are slightly longer. The furrows between the ribs are deep and narrow. This species is a quick grower.

Cereus jamacaru. S. America. This is a very

Plate 21. *Echinocereus pectinatus* in flower. P.64

Plate 22. *Echinocereus dasyacanthus* in flower. P.64

popular species with amateurs, and is easily grown. The stem is columnar, with 4 to 6 ribs, bluish-green when young but becoming dull green. The large greyish areoles bear numerous yellow spines of various lengths.

Cereus alacriportanus. Uruguay, Paraguay and S. Brazil. Has a bluish-green stem which later becomes deep green. The areoles are whitish and rather small, and bear 6 to 9 awl-shaped spines.

Cereus peruvianus. SW. Brazil and N. Argentina. A popular favourite, easy to cultivate in a rich calcareous soil. It has 5 to 8 ribs, thick and obtuse and slightly notched, with acute furrows between. The round, brownish areoles bear about 7 radial and 1 central spines the spines in the upper areoles being often more numerous.

MONVILLEA. In this genus, the species number 11. They have slender stems, long, more or less prostrate, with nocturnal flowers, and are natives of S. America.

Monvillea Cavendishii. S. Brazil, N. Argentina and Paraguay. This plant has slender stems, dark green with 9 obtuse ribs, which are somewhat warty. The areoles are small and whitish; radial spines number 7 to 9, and central spines 1 to 4. The plant is free flowering and bears white flowers.

Monvillea rhodoleucantha. A plant of easy cultivation requiring half shade. Very free flowering, and the flowers are very attractive, with pink outer petals and white inner petals. The areoles are small, whitish passing to brownish; radial spines number 6 or 7, centrals 1 to 3; all spines are at first yellowish-brown, changing to greyish, with a dark point.

CEPHALOCEREUS. In this genus there are quite a few species, including those that are tall, erect, columnar, and generally woolly or hairy at the areoles. At flowering time the flowering areoles develop an additional mass of wool or hair often referred to as a *pseudocephalium*, which hides the small, bell-shaped or funnel-shaped flowers. The plants are of easy cultivation in full sunshine, and they are very popular with collectors.

Cephalocereus senilis (Plate 13). The best-known species of the genus, this is often called the "old man cactus". It is a very attractive plant right from the seedling stage, though of slow growth. The stem is at first light green, becoming grey with age; the areoles are large, and the spines number 1 to 5. Along with the spines from each areole are developed from 20 to 30 long white hair-like soft bristles or hairs, which completely cover the plant.

Cephalocereus Hoppenstedtii. A very beautiful plant of slow growth and easy cultivation; a worthy companion to *C. senilis*.

ESPOSTOA. These are found in Ecuador and Northern Peru. They are columnar plants, hairy or woolly, developing a cephalium from the central axis. They are very popular with collectors. A suitable compost consists of 1 part loam, 1 part leaf-mould, 1 part sand, and a quarter part old mortar rubble.

Espostoa lanata. Branching above, dull grey-green, with rather sparse hairs, which become thicker at the crown. The areoles on the numerous ribs are very woolly at first, bearing about 12 yellow to reddish radial spines, and 1 or 2 clearly recognizable central spines, and much silky white hair entirely covering the stem. Flower, white or whitish-pink. This is a beautiful species which requires warmth, and thrives well in half shade or in full sunshine.

Espostoa Dautwitzii. Often considered as a variety of *E. lanata.* The ribs are more numerous and more acute. The areoles are yellow, furnished with very silky pale yellow hair, denser and longer at the top, but becoming lightly matted and covering the stem lower down. A cristate form is in cultivation.

OREOCEREUS. The genus includes 4 well-defined species, all natives of the Andes and of Bolivia and Peru. They make handsome plants, covered in longish hairs and bearing numerous strong, yellow spines, 2 inches in length. The flowers are dark red.

Oreocereus celsianus. A lovely species of rather slow growth, often branching from the base. The stems have 9 to 17 ribs; the areoles are woolly and whitish, bearing a cluster of slender yellowish-brown radial spines, and 1 to 4 centrals. The plant requires a compost consisting of 1 part silver sand, 1 part loam, and 1 part leaf soil, and should be freely watered during the warm weather.

Oreocereus Trollii. A low-growing species, the stem light green, with about 9 ribs. The large, oval areoles are furnished with creamy white or light grey wool, about 7 radial spines, and 1 to 3 central spines which are longer and stouter. Hairs, at first silky and creamy white, afterwards woolly and dirty white, entirely cover the stem. Popularly known as "the old man of the Andes", the plant is easily cultivated, and requires the same treatment as *O. celsianus.*

It will grow better when grafted on *Cereus* stock, but it has been noticed that it is not free flowering.

PACHYCEREUS. These are tall plants, branching at the base. Several species present a development of white, yellowish, or brownish wool from the areoles on the top of the plant or the flowering part of the stems. They seldom flower in cultivation, and the flowers are comparatively small.

Pachycereus Pringlei. Mexico and Lower California. The young plants are very attractive and easy to grow from seed. There are 10 to 16 ribs, with numerous spines on the large areoles; the central spines number 1 to 3, and are stronger and longer than the radials. This plant prefers a sandy soil in full sunshine.

Pachycereus chrysomallus. A beautiful species of slow growth, having 12 to 15 ribs. The radial spines number 8 to 10, with 1 to 3 central spines, which may reach a length of 5 to 6 inches. Creamy white flowers are produced near the top, beginning as compact masses of brownish wool which cover the ovary and the lower part of the flower.

LEMAIREOCEREUS. This genus includes 21 species, and is extensively grown. The plants are mostly tall with erect stems branching from the base. They grow well in a mixture of 1 part sharp sand, 1 part loam, and 1 part leaf-mould.

Lemaireocereus pruinosus. Central Mexico. Grows well from seed, producing good specimens in about three years. The stems are dull green, with 5 or 6 deep ribs. Radial spines number 8 to 9; central spines 1 to 4.

Lemaireocereus marginatus. Central and S. Mexico.

A beautiful and fast growing species, easily grown from seed, requiring full sunshine and warmth. Radial spines number 7, and centrals 1 or 2.

Lemaireocereus Beneckei. Central Mexico. In collections it forms an attractive column with 5 to 9 ribs, of which the growing top is a delightful sea-green, some parts of it having the appearance of being powdered. The areoles are at first white, becoming brownish, with about 5 radial spines and 1 central spine. Not an easy plant to grow on its own roots, it requires a soil rich in humus, but very porous, and must be given all the sunshine possible.

WILCOXIA. These are interesting plants, pretty and free flowering, requiring full sunshine. They are remarkable for the very large root tubers they produce, which resemble the tubers of dahlias.

Wilcoxia Poselgeri. Southern Texas and Mexico. Areoles very close together, very small and woolly; the radial spines are whitish or greyish, slender and hair-like, with 1 central spine. Flowers last in bloom for 4 to 5 days, and are pink, with reddish scales as well as bristles, and whitish hairs on the ovary and tube; the inner petals are narrower and darker pink.

Wilcoxia Schmollii. Mexico. Has 8 to 10 ribs, entirely hidden under a mass of whitish or greyish hairs, silky and spreading. The flowers are purplish-red or violet-red. A very desirable plant.

NYCTOCEREUS. There are 4 species in this genus which is native to Mexico and Central America. The stems are slender; when young they are erect, but afterwards trailing. The ribs are numerous, the areoles small, each with 10 or more slender spines. The flowers are large or medium, and borne at night along the sides of the stems. The growing stem finishes in a flower.

Nyctocereus serpentinus. Probably the most popular of the genus. The flower is large, nearly a foot long and over 7 inches wide, with delicate pink petals fading into soft cream-white; it has a strong fragrance with a pronounced spicy odour. This plant is often seen in collections.

HELIOCEREUS. This genus comprises 7 species, all of which are very beautiful and desirable. They are easily cultivated, and thrive well in half shade as well as in full sunshine. All the Heliocerei are warmth-loving plants and flower better in full sunshine, in a mixture of 2 parts leaf-mould, 1 part loam and 1 part crushed bricks.

Heliocereus speciosus. Central Mexico. Erect or trailing and freely branching, the growing top dark red or reddish, passing to dark green. The areoles are large and woolly, with 5 to 8 spines. The inner petals of the flower are a shiny carmine, and green at the base. This species has been used to produce some of the most beautiful hybrid Epiphyllums.

TRICHOCEREUS. This genus comprises over 28 species, mostly bearing superb flowers. The flowers are nocturnal, large, funnel-shaped, mostly white, and highly perfumed.

Trichocereus schickendantzii. Argentina. Thrives well in cultivation and is frequently seen in collections. It grows well from seed and forms erect columns of a shining dark green, with about 16 ribs. The areoles are yellowish-white, passing to brown; the spines yellowish. The pointed flower buds are covered with black wool and rise from the crowns

56

Plate 23. *Opuntia elata*. P.46

Plate 24. *Echinopsis* in flower. P.68

Plate 25. *Echinocactus ingens visnaga.* P.76
Ariocarpus retusus. P.70

Plate 26. Flowers of *Opuntia versicolor* (variable in colour). P.47

of the small columns, opening into large, very beautiful white funnel-shaped flowers, with a delicious perfume.

Trichocereus candicans. NW. Argentina. A robust species of easy cultivation, forming characteristic groups of branches from the base. It is shining green on top, dark green lower down, with 9 to 11 low ridges. The large areoles filled with white wool bear 10 to 14 radial spines, and thicker central spines.

Trichocereus macrogonus (Plate 13). Argentina and Bolivia. The stems are columnar, with 6 to 9 prominent rounded ribs with narrow furrows between them. The radial spines number 6 to 9, the thicker central spines 1 to 3; the flowers are large, greenish-white outside and white inside. This species is often used for grafting stock for Echinocacti, etc.

Trichocereus spachianus (Plate 14). A fine species, fast growing. The stems, freely branching from the base, are glossy light green, with 10 to 15 rounded ribs; the spines are yellow at first, passing to brown; radials 8, centrals 1 or 2. The flowers are produced near the top of the stem, the outside petals being greenish, the inner petals white. A night-flowering species.

HARRISIA is a genus of sub-tropical species with slender tall stems, with 5 to 11 ribs. The spines are variable, the flowers nocturnal, rather large, and borne near the top of the stems. The genus includes 19 species, many of which are popular with collectors.

Harrisia eriophora. Cuba. A species well suited to cultivation. The plant has 8 to 9 ribs, the areoles bearing 6 to 9 spines. The flower has a greenish tube, with petals reddish outside and white inside.

Harrisia gracilis. Jamaica. The stems are slender, dark green, with 9 to 11 ribs; the areoles have 10 to 16 spines. The flowers are brownish outside and white inside. This plant requires warmth, and water must be withheld in cold weather.

Harrisia Martinii (Plate 15). Argentina. The stems are branched, green passing to greyish-green; radial spines are very short, numbering 5 to 7, with 1 central spine. The flowers are very beautiful and freely produced, the outer petals being pale green with reddish tips, the inner petals white.

Harrisia Bonplandii (Plate 15). Brazil, Argentina and Paraguay. The stems are bluish-green, passing to greyish, with 4 to 6 ribs. The areoles are greyish and bear 3 to 5 grey spines. This species has unusually beautiful flowers, with the outer petals brownish-green, the inner petals white.

CLEISTOCACTUS. These plants have erect stems, mostly slender, and usually very spiny. The spines are frequently brightly coloured. The flowers are small, with a long narrow tube, brightly coloured orange to red, and freely produced over a long period. The species are native to South America, and are of easy cultivation, requiring full sunshine and frequent watering in the growing season. They are easily propagated from seed and are very popular with collectors. The genus consists of 6 species.

Cleistocactus Baumannii. Argentina. The stems are stiff, with 12 to 16 ribs. The areoles bear numerous white, yellow, or brown spines which, with the orange to scarlet flowers, make the whole an attractive combination.

Cleistocactus Strausii (Plate 16). Bolivia. A very

popular plant with collectors, and undoubtedly a lovely species. The slender, erect stem, branching from the base, is light green with approximately 25 ribs. The areoles have whitish wool, numerous hair-like white bristles, and about 4 yellow spines. A cristate form is also in cultivation.

CARNEGIEA. There is only one species in the genus, which is named in honour of Carnegie, the well-known American philanthropist. These wonderful giant cacti are indeed the silent sentinels of the desert. They are often referred to as "Sahuaro".

Carnegiea gigantea (Plate 57). Arizona and SE. California. The columnar stem, with 12 to 24 obtuse ribs, branches at 10 to 15 feet, and eventually grows to 30 to 50 feet. One of the largest of the cactus family, it attains a great age, often 250 years or more. It bears numerous awl-shaped spines, brown or greyish, with darker tips, thick and stiff; the radials are spreading, with 3 to 6 centrals which are thicker and longer. The flowers, produced near the top of mature plants, are greenish outside, white inside, and have numerous stamens with yellow anthers. Growth is very slow, so that specimens of a foot high are already of considerable age. Grows readily from seed.

LOPHOCEREUS. This is a genus of only one species. Columnar plants native to Sonora, Arizona, and Lower California, they are of slow growth but easy cultivation.

Lophocereus Schottii. The stems are dull green, erect and branching from the base, with 5 to 7 ribs. The areoles are large with 4 to 7 spines. The small pinkish flowers, which are nocturnal, are borne on the flowering tips, two or more from one areole, an exception to the general rule of one flower to an areole. There are three varieties of this plant, var. *australis*, var. *sargentianus*, and var. *Gatesii*.

Sub-Tribe II. HYLOCEREANAE

HYLOCEREUS. These can be described as forest climbing cacti. They have long snake-like branches studded with beautiful blossoms with red, purplish or greenish sepals, and with white petals. There are about 18 species. They prefer half shade and warmth and in summer-time liberal watering. The flowers are nocturnal.

Hylocereus undatus. West Indies. Famous for its very large blooms, it is commonly met with in cultivation. The stems are deep green, much branched and triangular; the spines very short and thick. Frequently used as grafting stock for *Zygocactus, Epiphyllum*, and *Rhipsalis*. Of easy cultivation in a mixture of 1 part loam, 1 part leaf-mould, and 1 part sand.

SELENICEREUS. The genus includes more than 20 species. Their flowers are probably the finest and the largest of all Cactaceae. They are nocturnal, or mostly so, strongly perfumed, and open towards sunset but wither off at sunrise. They are popularly named "Queen of the Night". Those who have seen these flowers in the fading light are struck by their unearthly radiance.

Selenicereus grandiflorus. West Indies. Often described as a marvel of the vegetable kingdom. The flowers have inspired both painters and poets of many countries. It is a climbing species with fairly thin snake-like branches, green to greyish-green in colour, with 8 ribs. The spines are short, yellow or brownish with white hairs. Cuttings are easily propagated and grow quickly when rooted. The plants require frequent watering throughout the summer. They should be grown in a compost consisting of 1 part leaf-mould, 1 part loam, and 1 part sand, to which has been added a small quantity of old mortar rubble.

Selenicereus Macdonaldiae. Uruguay and Argentina. A species frequently seen in cultivation, quick growing and much branched. The stems are dark shiny green, sometimes shaded dark purple, with 5 to 7 ribs. There are few spines. The flowers, which appear in June and July, are large and white, but have no fragrance.

Selenicereus pteranthus (Plate 17). Mexico. A magnificent species. The stiff stems have 4 to 5 angles, and are a dull glaucous green, flushed with purple. The areoles have short, white wool and very short, thick and stiff spines. Flowers creamy-white with long narrow sepals, purplish-yellow on the outside, expanding horizontally. A free-flowering species.

APOROCACTUS. The genus consists of 7 species. They have slender, trailing stems which hang down gracefully. The flowers are a rich red or carmine, and when in flower the plants are very beautiful. The blooms last three or four days. The plants respond well to a treatment of liquid fertilizer when buds begin to form. They are natives of Mexico and Central America.

Aporocactus flagelliformis. Usually referred to as the "rat's tail cactus" because of its pendent method of growth. It is common in collections, for it is easily cultivated in a mixture of 2 parts leaf-mould,

1 part loam, and 1 part sharp sand. It delights in full sun and should be watered liberally throughout the summer. The stems are shining green, but later turn greyish. Ribs number 10 to 24, with numerous minute areoles; spines radiate in clusters of 15 to 20.

Aporocactus flagriformis. Very similar to the preceding species, but with 7 to 10 ribs, and the areoles farther apart; radial spines number 6 to 8, centrals 2 or more.

Aporocactus martianus. The stems may be erect or sprawling, with 8 ribs; radial spines number about 8, central spines 3 to 4. The plant is very free flowering and the flowers a lively red.

Sub-Tribe III. ECHINOCEREANAE

ECHINOCEREUS. The genus comprises a large number of species (approximately 65). They are plants of low growth with erect or occasionally prostrate, cylindrical branches, growing singly or forming groups. They always have large and beautiful flowers. Most species grow in full sunshine but a few prefer half shade. They are natives of the western states of the U.S.A. and Mexico, and in cultivation should be grown in a mixture of 1 part loam, 1 part leaf soil, 1 part sharp sand, and a half part broken brick.

Echinocereus rigidissimus. The stem is stiff and erect, its peculiarity being that its spines are of different colours in horizontal layers around the plant, naturally indicating the age of the plant and suggesting the name of "rainbow cactus". The areoles are elongated and bear 16 to 20 radial spines which are spreading and comb-like. Flowers large, purplish or pink in colour.

Plate 27. *Echinocactus Grusonii*. P.76

Plate 28. *Notocactus scopa candida.* P.79
Astrophytum myriostigma. P.78

Echinocereus pentalophus. A species of easy cultivation. Stems have only 4 to 6 ribs, and very short white spines with brown points, 3 to 5 radials, no central spines. The plant is distinguished by its very large lilac or pink flowers.

Echinocereus Blanckii. An allied species to *E. pentalophus*, with prostrate branches, possessing 5 to 7 ribs with brownish spines growing from brownish areoles. The flowers are similar, but of a lighter shade and with narrower petals.

Echinocereus De Laetii. A beautiful plant, its columns 4 to 8 inches in height, with long, white, soft and even waxy hairs, which are really modified spines covering the whole plant, giving it a strong resemblance to the "old man cactus" (*Cephalocereus senilis*). The stems have 20 to 24 straight ribs; the areoles are large, with 18 to 36 radial spines and about 5 central spines. The plant requires full sunshine and an abundant supply of water in summer. Its pink flowers, when produced, are very large in relation to the size of the plant.

Echinocereus Fendleri (Plate 19). The stems are a dull green, with 9 to 12 ribs. Radial spines number 8 to 13, and are stout, spreading and occasionally comb-like in arrangement, pale yellow, usually tipped with brown; there may be 1 or 2 awl-shaped central spines, curving upwards. Flowers, pink, rose and rose-purple, nearly 4 inches long and 4 inches wide. It is a plant of rather slow growth, easily raised from seed.

Echinocereus stramineus. The stems are erect and stiff, branching from the base, pale green with 10 to 13 ribs, and deeply furrowed. Small white areoles bear about 10 radial spines, with 3 or 4 central spines. Flowers, purple, but sparingly borne.

Echinocereus knippelianus. Has a thick, dark green stem, with 5 to 7 ribs, bearing feeble short yellow spines. Flowers, dark brown outside, carmine-violet inside.

Echinocereus triglochidiatus (Plate 20). A most attractive species and easy to grow. The stems are globose to cylindrical, simple or clustered, with 5 to 14 ribs. Radial spines number 3 to 12. The flowers are funnel-shaped, scarlet to crimson, and remain open for several days.

Echinocereus pectinatus (Plate 21). Central Mexico. Often seen in collections. A free-flowering species, of easy cultivation. Stems roundish to cylindrical, branching from the base, with 20 obtuse ribs. Oval areoles bear about 25 radial spines, comb-like and spreading, and 2 to 6 very short central spines. The flowers are pink inside, with white hairs and spines outside.

Echinocereus Engelmannii (Plate 32). An interesting species from Mexico, California, Arizona, Nevada and Utah. A rather slow grower. The stems are usually erect and stiff, branching from the base, pale green, with 11 to 14 low obtuse ribs separated by narrow furrows. Large, round areoles, about $\frac{1}{3}$ inch apart; radial spines number 12, and are awl-shaped and angular; central spines, 4 or more, are angular and thick; flowers, purplish red.

Echinocereus Fitchii. Texas. Erect stems, dull green, branching from the base, with 12 to 14 ribs. The spines, numerous and yellowish, stand out from the plant. Very free flowering, the pink flowers borne at the top of the stem.

Echinocereus dasyacanthus (Plate 22). Mexico, New Mexico and Texas. A free-flowering plant with

64

stems branching at the base having 18 ribs. Radial spines number 20, central spines 3 to 7. The flower is striking, lemon-yellow, with red rings on a grey background.

Echinocereus viridiflorus. New Mexico. Stems cylindrical, freely branching from the base, dark green with 13 ribs. The spines are brightly coloured, consisting of 15 radial spines and 2 or 3 white or reddish central spines. The plant has small green flowers.

Echinocereus chloranthus. Mexico, Texas and New Mexico. Resembles *E. viridiflorus*, the main difference being in the flowers, which are rich brown. The spines are shorter, and not so brightly tipped with red. When not in bloom it is difficult to tell these two apart.

CHAMAECEREUS. This is one of the prettiest of the smaller cacti and very popular in collections. It is very free flowering, and a small plant may have as many as 15 to 20 flowers, which are orange or scarlet. Four or five flowers open at a time, the flowering period lasting for a few weeks. There is only one species in the genus, namely:

Chamaecereus Silvestrii. Argentina. It has short, cylindrical branches, which are creeping. From one single branch it is possible, within one year, to grow a large plant with 12 or more branches, and these will all produce flowers in the following spring. It is of easy cultivation and should not be absent from the smallest collections. Although there is only one species in the genus, there are a few varieties, all of which are beautiful.

REBUTIA. All species in this genus are well worth growing, for they are easily cultivated and have lovely flowers, freely produced, which make them popular cacti and in great demand. Being small, they are very useful for bowl gardens.

Rebutia minuscula. Argentina. Flowers in the spring with brilliant crimson funnel-shaped flowers, which are quite large in comparison with the plant itself. The stem has 16 to 20 ribs, with very short whitish spines arranged in groups of 25 to 30. The flowers appear from the base of the plant, curving gracefully upwards. It grows well in either half shade or full sunshine.

Rebutia Fiebrigii. Bolivia. A white spiny globe with far more spines than *R. minuscula*, but its flowers, though very similar, are somewhat smaller.

Rebutia deminuta. Argentina. Has 11 to 13 ribs. The spines number 10 to 12, and are sometimes white tipped with brown, or entirely brown. Flowers, orange-red with pink stamens. Of easy cultivation and very popular because it flowers freely.

Rebutia aureiflora. Argentina. This plant has beautiful golden-yellow or orange-yellow flowers.

Rebutia salmonea. Argentina. Flowers, salmon-pink and free flowering.

Rebutia spinosissima. Argentina. Numerous golden-brown spines and red flowers.

Rebutia pseudominuscula. Argentina. Very like *R. minuscula* but the flowers are a clearer red.

LOBIVIA. (An anagram of Bolivia, the home of most of the species, though some are found also in Peru and Argentina.) The plants are globular, the flowers rather large and funnel-shaped, with a short tube. There are at least 45 species in the genus, all easily cultivated and free flowering.

Plate 29. *Echinocereus Fendleri.* P.63

Plate 30. *Mammillaria* species. P.84
A typical *Mammillaria* in flower

Lobivia Pentlandii. Bolivia and Peru. Probably the best known species, it includes many varieties of desirable plants, spherical in shape, bright green, with 12 deep furrowed ribs. Radial spines number 7 to 12, of brownish colour; only 1 central spine. The flowers are borne on the side of the plant, and are orange-red to carmine.

Lobivia Cumingii. Bolivia and Peru. Differs from *L. Pentlandii* both in form and flower. It produces small glaucous-green globose bodies, whose tubercles run spirally in about 18 rows. Each tubercle bears about 20 straight marginal spines, with 2 to 8 slightly longer central spines. Flowers are borne on the sides or near the top, and are orange-red with a yellow tube. Easy to grow in cultivation and very free flowering.

Lobivia cinnabarina. Bolivia. A very beautiful species, the flowers remaining in bloom for three days. The stem is globular, and shining dark green, with 18 to 21 ribs. Radial spines number 8 to 10, central spines 2 to 3. The flowers are scarlet to carmine with dark red stamens.

Lobivia famatimensis. N. Argentina. A small plant. Ribs number 20, and are irregular and warty, with many whitish or yellowish short spines covering the stem. Very free flowering. The colour of the flower varies from yellowish-white to red.

Lobivia mistiensis. S. Peru. The stem is globular or conical, with 25 to 30 ribs. Radial spines number 7 to 9, and are spreading. The flowers are pink.

Lobivia hertrichiana. Peru. Easily grown from seed. The stems are glossy pale green, with about 11 ribs. Radial spines number 7, with only 1 central spine. An excellent beginner's plant, flowering from quite young.

MEDIOLOBIVIA. Only a few species comprise this genus. They usually grow in tufts with globular stems. The flowers are large and yellow, with a slender hairy and scaly tube.

Mediolobivia duursmaiana. Argentina. The stems are a dark leaf-green, with many areoles bearing 10 thin radial spines and 1 central spine tipped with yellow. Flowers funnel-shaped, orange-yellow with a white throat.

Mediolobivia elegans. Argentina. The stems are pale green. Radial spines are whitish-yellow, and number about 14; central spines number 3 to 4, and are darker at the base. Flowers large, and bright yellow, with a slender tube and narrow petals.

ECHINOPSIS (Plate 24). These are very popular plants in collections and very suitable for cultivation on window-sills. They are endemic to the southern half of S. America, to the east of the Andes, which they have apparently not been able to cross. The plants are short, and cylindrical or globose in shape. The genus includes about 36 species. Although they love plenty of light, they should, during spring and summer, be given a little shade during the brightest hours of the day. They are easily cultivated, requiring a moderately rich compost of 1 part loam, 1 part leaf soil, 1 part sharp sand, and if a little old cow manure can be obtained, a half part can be added to the compost. Established plants produce off-sets, and often these are already rooted on the plant. They are easily separated and should be potted up and grown on to produce specimen plants.

Echinopsis multiplex. S. Brazil. Globular stems, with 12 to 15 slightly wavy ribs. Brown spines;

radials numbering 8 to 10, and centrals 2 to 5. The flowers are magnificent and fragrant, flesh-coloured, shading to pink at the point. There are many hybrids of this species.

Echinopsis eyriesii. Brazil, Uruguay and Argentina. Frequently found in collections. The stems are globular, and produce a host of young plants along the ribs. The spines of this species are very short, and number about 14. The flowers are borne on the sides of the plant, and are similar to *E. multiplex*, but are white.

Echinopsis rhodotricha. NE. Argentina and Paraguay. A very free-flowering species with dark green oval or cylindrical stems, sprouting at the base, and having 8 to 13 ribs. Radial spines number 4 to 7, with 1 central spine, but this is, however, often absent. The spines are yellow and somewhat curved. The plant bears slender white flowers, at the base of which are scales with red woolly hairs.

Echinopsis turbinata. S. Brazil and Argentina. The stem is dark green, globular or conical, and sprouting at the base, and has 13 or 14 ribs. Radial spines number 10 to 12, and are at first yellowish-brown, changing to horny brown; there are 6 central spines, very short and stiff, black or dark brown. The flower is funnel-shaped, with a green tube, the outer petals being dark green, the inner petals white with a greenish mid-rib.

Echinopsis decaisneana. Has large and beautiful red flowers. Easy to grow from seed and a desirable plant.

Echinopsis tubiflora. S. Brazil and Argentina. Stems globular, with age cylindrical, dark green; ribs 11 to 12, notched with acute furrows between them; radial spines numerous, yellowish and brown at tips; central spines 3 or 4 and stronger; outer petals of flower green, tipped brown, inner petals white with a green mid-rib on the dorsal side. Three varieties are in cultivation: var. *nigrispina*, var. *paraguayensis*, and var. *Graessneriana*. These are all popular beginner's plants. The distinguishing feature is the long tube of the flower. They do well in a living-room and will flower when about 3 inches in diameter.

Sub-Tribe IV. ECHINOCACTANAE

The plants in this sub-tribe are spherical or elongated. As a rule they are small plants of low habit. The flowers are developed singly on the areoles near the centre of the crowns, and are mostly funnel-shaped with a short tube. Many of the genera are heavily spined.

ARIOCARPUS. These are plants with a tap root, of low growth, round, flat-topped, and spineless. The tubercles have the appearance of thick triangular fleshy leaves. There are 7 species in the genus.

Ariocarpus retusus (Plate 25). Mexico. Forms a somewhat flattened grey-green to reddish rosette, about 5 inches in diameter. The crown of the plant is very woolly. The tubercles are more or less triangular; they are arranged in rosette form, and generally have a woolly, horny point. The flowers are white, with pink on the outside, and arise from the axils of younger tubercles.

Ariocarpus fissuratus. Texas and Mexico. The plant owes its name to its more or less warted and split exterior. It is approximately circular in shape and rarely exceeds 6 inches in diameter. The triangular tubercles form a rosette. The flowers are white to purple. Because of the plant's dull grey to brownish colour, which makes it difficult to distinguish from rocky surroundings, it is often called the "living rock cactus".

OBREGONIA. Includes only one species.

Obregonia denegrii. Mexico. A very striking plant resembling an artichoke in appearance. The tubercles are leaf-like, arranged spirally, and bear the areoles at their tops. These are at first woolly and then bear 2 to 4 delicate and somewhat curved spines. After a time, however, the spines and wool disappear. Free flowering and easy to grow.

LOPHOPHORA. The genus includes 2 or 3 species, which are much sought after by collectors. They form round bodies and are spineless, with flat ribs bearing tubercles with the areoles, each tufted with hairs.

Lophophora Williamsii (Plate 36). Central Mexico to S. Texas. The areoles bear papery tufts. The body of the plant is a glaucous green with a much thickened tap root. Ribs number 7 to 13. The flowers are pale pink, and appear at the centre of the plant. This peculiar plant has for centuries past played a part in the religious ceremonies and dances of certain North American Indian tribes.

AZTEKIUM. The genus consists of one species.

Aztekium Ritteri. Mexico. A globular plant with 8 to 11 ribs. Spines number 1 to 4. The flowers appear from the new areoles; their outer petals are white with a reddish band, and the inner petals are plain white.

EPITHELANTHA. The genus includes one species.

Epithelantha micromeris. Texas and N. Mexico. A beautiful plant with white closely set spines, it rarely exceeds $2\frac{1}{2}$ inches in diameter. It forms compact groups of small spherical stems, depressed at the top. The white to pale pink flowers are produced at the crown in a mat of wool and spines. It requires warmth and sunshine, and the soil mixture should be a rich calcareous one.

HAMATOCACTUS. This genus includes 3 species, and of these there are a number of varieties. The plants are globular or elongated. The central spines are long, and at least one of them is sharply hooked at the tip.

Hamatocactus Setispinus. Texas and N. Mexico. This strongly armed cactus attains a height of about 6 inches. Ribs number 13, radial spines 12 to 15, centrals 1 to 3. The flower is funnel-shaped, about 3 inches in length, whitish-yellow with a red centre.

LEUCHTENBERGIA. There is only one species in this genus.

Leuchtenbergia principis. Central and N. Mexico. This is undoubtedly the queerest cactus in the Echinocactus group. It has a long tap root. The tubercles are finger-shaped, and the plant possesses a thick woody stem which never branches but forms groups by producing young plants at the base. The areoles are at the tips of the tubercles, and bear papery spines, 8 to 14 radials and 1 to 2 centrals. The flowers are large, yellow and scented, and will last several days.

STENOCACTUS. The genus comprises 30 species. The plants are rather small with numerous thin ribs, which are often wavy. The flowers are small, pink, or greenish-pink or greenish-yellow with a short tube. Specimens are sought after by keen collectors.

Stenocactus multicostatus. Mexico. A very interesting species possessing about 100 wavy ribs, each bearing a few areoles producing 6 to 9 spines each, 3 long ones pointing upwards, and 4 to 6 pointing downwards. The flowers are whitish.

Stenocactus crispatus. Mexico. Ribs number about 25. Radial spines number 7 to 8 with only 1 central spine, which is stiff and straight. The pretty flowers have white outer petals with a broad violet-brown stripe and a violet edge. The other petals are violet with a carmine band.

FEROCACTUS. These plants can be described as powerful cacti, for they have exceptionally strong, heavy spines, and the name is suggestive of the ferocity of these weapons of defence. The stems are round or cylindrical. As a rule the areoles are large and the flowers are produced on the young areoles immediately above the groups of spines. They are mostly yellow or red. The genus includes about 32 species.

Ferocactus acanthodes. S. California. The stem of this plant generally grows singly, and with age can attain a height of about 9 feet and reach 1 foot in diameter. Radial spines number 9 to 13, centrals 4. The flowers are shades of yellow and orange. Grows well in cultivation, particularly in sunny exposures, and is a desirable species.

Ferocactus Wislizenii (Plate 39). Texas and Arizona. When young the stem is globular, becoming cylindrical with age. It is a very fine plant, growing to a height of 7 feet. Ribs number 15 to 25. The areoles are large and oval, and at first bear yellowish wool, which turns brown or grey; radial spines number about 20, centrals 4, the latter very thick and strongly hooked at the tip. The flowers have a green tube, with the outer petals green, the inner petals reddish-yellow. Grows well in cultivation, requiring sunshine and warmth and a rich porous soil to which has been added some gravel, chippings or crushed bricks, and a small quantity of old mortar rubble.

Ferocactus Pringlei. Mexico. One of the largest species of *Ferocactus.* Individual plants in the wild may reach a height of 9 to 10 feet with a diameter of 12 to 16 inches. Possesses 16 to 18 ribs with numerous closely set areoles, the outer edges of which show a row of long yellow or straw-coloured hairs or bristles, with a few needle-shaped spines. There is 1 central spine, which is the strongest and is somewhat flattened and generally curved, though sometimes practically straight. The species has red flowers, with yellow inside. It is a desirable plant when young, and should be included in all collections.

Ferocactus latispinus. Mexico. Perhaps one of the best known of the genus. It has 8 to 14 ribs when young, and 21 ribs when old. Radial spines number 6 to 10, central spines 4. The flowers are normally pink or purplish-red, but frequently shades of mauve and deep violet-blue.

ECHINOMASTUS. The genus includes 7 species. They are small, with globular or short cylindrical stems, well provided with spines and with low ribs.

Echinomastus Macdowellii. N. Mexico. A beautiful species with a pale green stem entirely covered with long white spines. Ribs number 20 to 25. The areoles are furnished with white wool; radial spines number 15 to 20, central spines 3 to 4. The flowers are pink,

Echinomastus erectocentrus. The stem grows singly, and is bluish-green, with 20 or more ribs, arranged spirally. The grey-green areoles are set closely together; radial spines number about 16, and there is only 1 central spine. The flowers are reddish-purple and formed at the top of the stem. A handsome species which grows easily from seed. The plants thrive well in full sunshine in a mixture of leaf-mould, loam and chippings, in equal parts.

GYMNOCALYCIUM. This genus forms a remarkable group of spherical cacti, which may be recognized from the more or less distinct "chin" or chin-shaped extension below the areoles. The spines are spreading, and sometimes recurved, suggesting in certain species a kind of spider. This is noticeable, especially on *G. denudatum*, which is sometimes nicknamed the "spider cactus".

Gymnocalycium denudatum. S. Brazil, Uruguay, and Argentina. This plant has 5 to 8 very broad ribs, only slightly notched, with the chin below the areoles hardly pronounced. Spines number 5 to 8; there are no central spines. The flowers are green, margined with white, the inner petals white or pink with a green band.

Gymnocalycium saglione. N. Argentina. The dull green stems are globular, with 10 to 13 ribs according to the age of the plant. While young, the areoles are felty and at first have erect spines which later bend outwards. Radial spines number 7 to 12, centrals 3. The flower has a short tube, green outside, white or pale pink inside. This plant is frequently found in collections, and is easy to grow but requires half shade.

Gymnocalycium platense. Argentina. The stems are globular, glaucous green, possessing 12 to 14 ribs. The chins below the areoles are prominent. Radial spines number about 7; there are no centrals. Flowers greyish-green, white inside. This is a beautiful species, easy to grow and very free flowering.

ECHINOCACTUS. The genus contains some interesting plants, with globular or small columnar ovoid stems, forming plump cacti. The spines are numerous and strong. The flowers are borne on the young areoles, and are usually yellow in colour.

Echinocactus Grusonii (Plate 27). Central Mexico. A very popular plant with growers, found in most collections. The light green stems are solitary, globose or cylindrical according to age, and the ribs may vary in number from 20 to 30. When young the spines are pale golden-yellow, turning almost white as plants get older. Radial spines number 8 to 10, central spines 3 to 5. The flowers are yellow and open during sunshine, but are never fully open.

Echinocactus ingens. Mexico. The stem is globular or elongated, sea-green with purplish brown shading, and very woolly at the top. This is one of the largest of the spherical cacti. In young plants, the ribs number 5 to 8, but old plants possess many ribs. The areoles are large, with abundant yellowish wool, each bearing 8 radial spines and 1 central spine. The flowers are reddish-yellow outside and yellow inside.

Echinocactus ingens visnaga (Plate 25). Young plants are globular, but they become elongated with age. The plants are greyish-green with tawny wool at the top. There are up to 40 ribs with roundish or elongated areoles bearing pale brown-ringed spines, 4 thick and 6 thin, spreading crosswise; the upper part of the spine is thick and long. Flowers, yellow.

Echinocactus horizonthalonius. Texas, New Mexico to Arizona and N. Mexico. This is a small and beautiful species. The pale sea-green stem is solitary, globular or cylindrical, with 7 to 13 ribs, rounded and frequently spirally arranged. The areoles are woolly and contain 6 to 9 spines; the single central spine, when present, is even stronger than the marginal ones. The flower is beautiful, pale pink in colour, and striking against the sea-green stem.

ASTROPHYTUM. The genus consists of 4 species, with numerous varieties. The stems are globular, with the ribs very pronounced and covered with minute star-like scales. The plants grow well in a sandy compost rich in lime. Great care should be exercised in winter to see that they are kept dry. In summer they enjoy full sunshine and frequent watering. All are of easy cultivation, and worth acquiring.

Astrophytum asterias. Mexico. The stem is flat and dome-shaped, with 8 ribs, the areoles woolly and quite spineless. The flowers are large, yellow, and reddish at the centre, and appear at the top of the centre of the plant.

Astrophytum capricorne. New Mexico. The whole plant is covered with woolly scales. Ribs number 8. The large areoles contain brownish wool, with a variable number of long, twisted spines. The flowers are very beautiful, yellow with a reddish-orange blotch at the base, and open wide. There are several varieties of this species, any of which is worth acquiring.

Astrophytum myriostigma (Plate 28). Central Mexico. A very popular cactus. The stem is globular and slightly depressed at the centre, and covered with scales which give it a greyish stone-like appearance. The number of ribs varies from 4 to 8. Spines are absent. The flowers develop from the centre of the plant, and are plain yellow, or yellow with a reddish blotch at the base. Of easy cultivation, and enjoys full sunshine. There are quite a number of varieties of this species.

Astrophytum ornatum. Central Mexico. This plant possesses sharp, awl-shaped spines, radiating in all directions. The stem is studded with scales larger than in any of the other species, and has 8 angular ribs, often twisted. The flowers are large and lemon-yellow.

NOTOCACTUS. The genus includes 25 species, all of which are beautiful plants.

Notocactus concinnus. S. Brazil and Uruguay. The stem is globular, glossy green, depressed at the top with about 18 ribs. Radial spines number 10 to 12, central spines 4. The flowers appear at the top of the plant, the outer petals being red with a darker dorsal band, the inner petals canary-yellow. It is a free-flowering plant requiring full sunshine.

Notocactus Leninghausii. S. Brazil. The stem is cylindrical, with about 30 ribs. Radial spines number about 15; central spines 3 or 4. The flowers appear at the top of the plant, the outer petals being greenish, the inner petals yellow. This is a very

Plate 31. *Mammillaria Parkinsonii*. P.85
Mammillaria pusilla. P.86

Plate 32. Flowers of *Echinocereus Engelmannii*. P.64

popular cactus, requiring half shade and moderate watering.

Notocactus Graessneri. S. Brazil. An interesting species. The globular stem is flattened and depressed at the top, with 50 to 60 ribs arranged spirally. The areoles have yellow wool and numerous spines, of which the 5 or 6 centrals are thicker. Flowers appear at the top of the plant, and are greenish-yellow. Of easy cultivation in half shade.

Notocactus scopa (Plate 28). S. Brazil and Uruguay. A lovely species entirely covered with white spines. Ribs number 30 to 35; radial spines about 40; central spines 3 to 4. The flowers appear at the centre, and are yellow. This plant requires full sunshine and the compost should be rich. During the summer season it should be freely watered, but care must be exercised to keep the plant dry in winter.

Notocactus tabularis. Uruguay and S. Brazil. The bluish-green stem is globular or elongated, with 16 to 23 ribs. Radial spines number 16 to 18, central spines 4. The flower is glossy yellow with a carmine throat. The species is easy to grow and free flowering but does best in half shade.

Notocactus muricatus. Uruguay and S. Brazil. The stem is pale green, globular or elongated, with about 20 ribs. Radial spines number 15, central spines 3 to 4. The flower is pale yellow. This species requires full sunshine and is not difficult to grow.

Notocactus apricus. Uruguay. A very popular plant requiring full sunshine. It is easy to grow, and will flower readily. The globular, pale green stem has 15 to 20 ribs, slightly notched; radial spines number 18 to 20, centrals 4. The flowers are large and yellow, with the outer petals reddish on the dorsal side.

Notocactus floricomus. Uruguay. The stem is globular, with 20 ribs. Spines number 20, with 4 or 5 spreading central spines. The yellow flowers are produced freely. The plant is of rather slow growth and does best in half shade.

Notocactus pampeanus. Uruguay and Argentina. Has a dark green stem, globular, elongating with age, having 21 ribs. Radial spines number 7 to 10, and are yellow in colour; 1 central spine. Flowers, yellow.

Notocactus Ottonis. S. Brazil, Uruguay, Paraguay and Argentina. One of the most beautiful species of the genus. An excellent plant for beginners, it flowers freely, requiring half shade. The stem is solitary, or sprouting from the base, globular or elongated, with 10 to 13 ribs. Radial spines number 10 to 18, central spines 3 or 4. The flower is glossy yellow, and the stigma has 14 dark red lobes.

Varieties of this species are: var. *tenuispinus,* var. *tortuosus,* var. *paraguayensis,* var. *uruguayensis,* var. *linkii,* var. *brasiliensis.*

Notocactus Haselbergii. S. Brazil. A deservedly popular cactus having a globular stem, flat and depressed at the top and entirely covered with white spines. The areoles contain white wool, and bear about 20 radial spines and 3 to 5 central spines. The outer petals of the flower are red, the inner petals orange-red. Flowers last for over a week. Of easy cultivation, requiring half shade.

PARODIA. The genus comprises small plants which are globular or have elongated stems. There are 18 listed species.

Parodia chrysacanthion. Argentina. Stem pale green with 24 ribs arranged spirally. The spreading spines number 30 or 40, and are whitish-yellow to golden-yellow. The flowers appear at the top of the plant and are golden-yellow. This plant requires half shade and grows well in 1 part loam, 1 part soil, 1 part sand.

Parodia Stuemeri. Argentina. The pale green stems are globular, with 20 ribs. Radial spines number 25, central spines 4. The flower is golden-yellow, with the tips of the petals orange with brown.

Parodia microsperma. Argentina. The globular, light green stem, branching from the base, has numerous ribs bearing small woolly areoles; radial spines number 10 to 20, central spines 3 or 4. The flowers are funnel-shaped, with the outer petals red, the inner petals orange-yellow. The species requires half shade.

Parodia nivosa. A lovely species requiring full sunshine. It has numerous ribs. Radial spines number 10 to 20, central spines about 4. The flowers are scarlet.

Parodia mutabilis. Argentina. The stems are globular, glaucous green with white wool at the top; the ribs are indistinct. Radial spines number about 45, central spines 3 or 4. The flowers are golden-yellow. The species is very variable, but none the less beautiful.

Parodia sanguiniflora. Argentina. Has a solitary globular stem, green with a woolly top. Radial spines number about 15, central spines 4. The flowers are blood-red. One of the prettiest of the Parodias.

Sub-Tribe v. CACTANAE

DISCOCACTUS. The plants in this genus are small, globular, and more or less flattened. The flowers are nocturnal and there are 7 species.

Discocactus Hartmannii. The stems are globular and glossy green. Radial spines number about 12, with 1 central spine. The petals are white with greenish-white bracts with darker mid-rib.

CACTUS. The genus includes about 20 species. They are natives of the West Indies and S. America, and are distinguished when adult by a singular woolly or bristly body termed the *cephalium* or head, which is formed on the crown of the globose plant. This cephalium is a form of terminal flowering branch with a woody centre, and grows to a considerable height. The flowers are invariably small and pink.

Cactus intortus. West Indies. The body of this plant is at first spherical but subsequently becomes cylindrical. The cephalium is round, flat at first, and completely covered with white wool and soft brown bristles. Ribs number 14 to 20; spines 10 to 15. Flowers, pink.

Discocactus and *Cactus* genera are not easy to grow, for they require more heat than the majority of other cacti.

Sub-Tribe VI. CORYPHANTHANAE

This sub-tribe consists of low spiny plants, mostly globular, but sometimes cylindrical. They have numerous tubercles and these are usually arranged spirally. The flowers may be large or small according to the species.

THELOCACTUS. The genus includes 25 species of globular plants, sometimes very spiny.

Thelocactus bicolor. S. Texas to Central Mexico.

Plate 33. *Echinocereus pectinatus.* P.64

Plate 34. *Mammillaria saetigera*. P.87
Mammillaria gracilis. P.87

The stem is usually solitary, globular to oval, but sometimes cylindrical, with 8 ribs. Radial spines number 9 to 18, central spines 4; the flowers are large and violet-red.

Thelocactus wagnerianus. W. Mexico. The stem is cylindrical, with 13 ribs. Radial spines number about 20, spreading comb-like, with only 1 central spine. The spines are red, or yellow and red. This species sometimes produces young plants at the base.

Thelocactus gielsdorfianus. Mexico. The greyish-green stem is solitary, globular to oval, with the ribs divided into broad angular warts. The areoles bear 6 to 7 spreading spines. The plant is free flowering, with white flowers.

Thelocactus nidulans. Mexico. The stem is solitary with about 20 ribs divided into acute warts. The spines number about 15, and are so grouped and arranged that they look like a bird's nest. This is a fine species with pale yellow flowers.

CORYPHANTHA. The genus comprises over 50 species, all possessing large flowers. Their cultivation is easy, and they appreciate full sunshine at all times.

Coryphantha deserti. Arizona, S. California, and Nevada. A very beautiful species. The stem is solitary, but sprouts at the base when adult. Radial spines are numerous, with 10 central spines. The flowers are a pale red.

Coryphantha recurvata. Arizona and N. Mexico. The plant forms clusters with globular stems. The comb-like radial spines number 20 to 25, central spines 1 or 2. The flowers are yellow and brown.

Coryphantha Palmeri. Mexico. This is another lovely globular cactus with closely set tubercles. Spreading radial spines number 11 to 14, with 1 central spine. The flowers are yellowish-white with a brown mid-rib, and appear at the crown.

Coryphantha radians. Mexico. The stem is solitary, globular, but sometimes elongated. There are up to 20 white to yellowish radial spines, all spreading, but no central spine. The flowers are lemon-yellow, with the outer petals tipped with red.

Coryphantha aggregata (Plate 42). Arizona and New Mexico. The globular or cylindrical stem, 2 to 3 inches in diameter, eventually forms clusters up to about 15 inches across. The tubercles are arranged spirally in 15 to 17 rows, with 15 to 40 radial spines, about $\frac{1}{2}$ inch long; 6 central spines spread out in a brush, especially in more mature plants. The spines are white, tipped reddish-brown. The beautiful bright pink to rose-purple flowers, each 2 to 3 inches in diameter, are arranged round the centre of the plant. Seeds germinate readily.

MAMMILLARIA (Plate 30). The genus is a large one with over 200 species. They are mostly natives of Mexico and are favoured plants in collections. Many are easily grown from seed and, although the flowers are not large, a number appear in a ring around the top of the plant, and usually last for some days. Most species prefer full sunshine, but there are a few that grow best in half shade, especially during the bright days of summer. Besides their pretty flowers, they produce fruits, mostly red.

Mammillaria elongata. W. Mexico. Forms clusters with stems which are generally cylindrical and erect, but sometimes prostrate. This species is very easy to grow and popular in collections. There are a number of varieties, all of which are worth while growing, particularly var. *echinata*, var. *rufocrocea*, and var. *stella-aurata*.

Mammillaria microhelia. Mexico. A very beautiful species preferring full sunshine. The stem is solitary or sprouting, with short tubercles. Radial spines number about 50, central spines 1 to 4. The flowers are creamy-white.

Mammillaria plumosa. N. Mexico. A beautiful species, forming clusters entirely covered with feathery spines. The flowers are white, with a brown or reddish mid-rib. The plant is of easy cultivation in full sunshine. Watering should be frequent in the growing season, but in winter the plant should be kept dry.

Mammillaria kewensis. Mexico. An interesting species having 5 or 6 brown radial spines fixed in star fashion on the tubercles, there being no central spine. The flowers are purple.

Mammillaria Heyderi. N. Mexico, Texas. An attractive plant with a flattened hemispherical stem, and conical, angular tubercles. The bristle-like radial spines are white with brown tips and number 20, the outer ones long. There is 1 central spine. Flowers red, with dark central bands.

Mammillaria camptotricha. Mexico. Spherical with dark green stems, forming large clumps. Spines number 4 or 5. The outer petals of the flowers are greenish, the inner petals white. The plant is easily cultivated and deservedly popular.

Mammillaria Parkinsonii (Plate 31). Central Mexico. The sea-green stems are somewhat compressed, conical to cylindrical in shape. Radial spines number 20 to 30, with 2 central spines, tipped with dark brown. The flowers are small and yellowish. A very beautiful plant, often seen in collections.

Mammillaria hahniana. Mexico. One of the most beautiful of the Mammillarias, it has a globular stem, rather flattened on top, with silky white hairs which give the plant a singular appearance. Radial spines number about 30; there are 2 central spines, which are straight and erect. The crimson flowers are arranged in a ring around the top of the plant.

Mammillaria rhodantha. Mexico. The species has a dark green cylindrical stem, which forms large clumps with age. Radial spines number 16 to 20; central spines 4 to 6. The flowers are numerous, the outer petals reddish-brown with a white margin, the inner petals carmine-red. There are numerous beautiful varieties, and all are of easy cultivation.

Mammillaria celsiana. Mexico. The stem is solitary, globular to cylindrical, rather flat on top and well furnished with white wool. Radial spines number 20 to 26, central spines 4. The flowers are produced in a ring at the top of the plant, the outer petals reddish-brown, the inner petals pink to carmine. A very lovely species thriving best in half shade.

Mammillaria bombycina. Mexico. The stem is globular, becoming cylindrical with age, with blunt tubercles arranged in spirals, and conspicuous for their white wool. Radial spines number 30 to 40, central spines 4. The flowers are clear red.

Mammillaria pusilla (Plate 31). More commonly named *M. prolifera*. Clusters freely, making a fine pot plant. The dark green stems, soft in texture, are globular or short and cylindrical, with tubercles closely set in spirals of 5 and 8. Central spines number 5 to 9, with up to 40 radial spines. The outer petals of the flowers are greenish-yellow, while the inner petals are broader and paler. The following varieties are in cultivation: var. *haitensis*, var. *texana*, var. *multiceps*.

Mammillaria saetigera (Plate 34). A globose species with the apex somewhat sunken. The tubercles are loosely arranged in 13 and 21 spirals, and glossy dark green. The areoles are elliptical with white wool only in the youngest. The axils have white wool, and also white bristles, especially in the lower part of the plant. Central spines number 2, radial spines 15 to 20. The flowers are white with a rose mid-stripe, the inner petals being darker.

Mammillaria gracilis (Plate 34). Forms clusters with cylindrical stems of a fresh green. The areoles are slightly woolly and bear 12 to 14 radial spines, which are yellowish-white at first, passing to white, stiff, and radiating star-like over the tubercles; central spines number 3 to 5. The flowers are yellowish-white. Two varieties are in cultivation: var. *fragilis* and var. *pulchella*.

Mammillaria microcarpa (Plate 47). One of the best of the Mammillarias. The stem is solitary, globose to cylindrical, rounded at the apex, with the tubercles arranged in 13 and 21 spirals. The stem is firm in texture, becoming corky with age, and a dark greyish-green. Central spines number 1 to 3, radial spines 20 to 30, and are white to dark yellow with a brown tip. The outer petals of the flowers are greenish with a tan mid-stripe, darker at the tip, and have pale green margins, with a tinge of pink;

the inner petals are pink, with darker mid-stripe and very pale margins.

Other species to be recommended are: *M. erythrosperma*, *M. Wildii*, *M. kunzeana*, *M. Schelhasei*, *M. decipiens*, *M. candida*.

DOLICHOTHELE.

This is a small genus of globular plants, solitary or clustering. They have thick roots. The flowers are very large, and yellow.

Dolichothele longimamma. Central Mexico. A very free-flowering species, popular with collectors. Radial spines number 5 to 7; central spines 1 to 3. The flowers are funnel-shaped, with the outer petals greenish-yellow and the inner petals canary-yellow. The plant has long cylindrical, more or less sea-green tubercles. There are several varieties of this species.

Dolichothele sphaerica. N. Mexico and S. Texas. A clustering plant, with pale green stems, more or less globular. Radial spines number 9 to 15, with 1 central spine. The beautiful flowers are sulphur-yellow.

Sub-Tribe VII. EPIPHYLLANAE

The sub-tribe consists mostly of epiphytic plants which, in their natural environment, grow on trees or on the ground. They are generally spineless, with many stems or branches. The flowers are usually large and showy.

ZYGOCACTUS.

There is one species in this genus.

Zygocactus truncatus. W. Brazil. It is built up of short, flat, thin joints, which generally hang down forming an umbrella shape. There are many varieties, the flowers varying from carmine to white. The joints are spineless and glossy green. The taxonomist now recognizes plants grown under this name as *Schlumbergera Bridgesii*. A very popular plant with the windowsill collector, often called the "Christmas cactus". Cultivation as for Epiphyllums.

SCHLUMBERGERA. The plants in this genus include two species with a similar habit of growth to Zygocactus. Both are natives of Brazil.

Schlumbergera Gaertneri. A free-flowering species, even when quite young. The scarlet flowers are borne in spring on the top areoles.

EPIPHYLLUM. Most of the Epiphyllums grow on trees in the wild state. They have flattened leaf-like stems a foot or more in length. The flowers are very large and a beautiful trumpet shape, between 3 and 7 inches across; the hybrids are in a wide range of colours, and are a sight when in flower. By means of hybridization of species, an extraordinary number of most beautiful plants have been produced (Plate 54). Those who have not seen them in flower before are often surprised at their beauty. Most kinds open their flowers in the evening and fade about 48 hours later, but as large plants produce a number of buds, the succession of opening flowers may last for about a fortnight.

The season of flowering depends on the temperature of the place in which they are grown, but May is the usual time.

After flowering, the plants should be rested for six weeks, and during this period only sufficient moisture given to prevent the soil drying out completely. At all other times the compost should never be allowed to become too dry. Watering should be less frequent in autumn and winter, and never water in really cold weather. It is beneficial to the plants if they can be placed out of doors for the summer months. Overhead spraying at each watering is appreciated.

A suitable compost in which to grow them is 3 parts leaf-mould, 1 part loam, 1 part sharp sand, and a sprinkling of bone meal. Re-potting should be done in August or September.

Epiphyllum Ackermanii (Plate 64). The plant known as such may be a hybrid but is certainly the most common and widespread of all the Epiphyllums. It has fleshy joints, sometimes three-angled. Flowers, large, funnel-shaped; petals, salmon-red with white stamens. Very free flowering.

Sub-Tribe VIII. RHIPSALIDANAE

This sub-tribe contains many interesting plants. They develop many-branched stems, and in their natural environment they are found growing on trees, or on the ground, in rocky places, from which they hang down. The branches or joints may be cylindrical, or flat and leaf-like, or angular. The spines are mostly absent. The flowers are small, and the berries which are produced are usually the prettiest decoration of the plant. They are white, red, or purple.

ERYTHRORHIPSALIS. This genus differs from *Rhipsalis* by the minute areoles which are furnished with bristle-like spines. There is only one species in the genus

Erythrorhipsalis pilocarpa. W. Brazil. A very

pretty species with thin cylindrical branches. The areoles have 3 to 10 greyish bristle-like spines. The berries are wine-red and furnished with bristles.

RHIPSALIS. The genus comprises about 58 species. Being Epiphytes, they require a fairly rich compost and must be grown in rather humid conditions and in shade. They enjoy frequent spraying.

Rhipsalis paradoxa. W. Brazil. A rather curious species. The branches, sometimes 4 feet in length, are formed of regular joints and look as if composed of pale green three-winged links. The flowering areoles are woolly and bristly when young. The flowers are white and the berries reddish.

Rhipsalis houlletiana. W. Brazil. The branches are leaf-like, flat and thin, the margins being dentate, with pointed teeth. Flowers bell-shaped, yellowish-white, with greenish tips. The berries are round and red.

Rhipsalis warmingiana. E. Brazil. A much-branched plant. The stems are long, broad, flat, or with three or four angles. The outer petals of the flower are green, the inner petals white. The berry is dark violet.

Rhipsalis salicornioides (Plate 35), also known as *Hariota salicornioides*. An erect bush, much branched. The joints are bottle-shaped, green, in whorls of 3 to 5. The areoles have short, white bristles. Flowers, yellow.

THE OTHER SUCCULENT
PLANTS

SUCCULENT plants, other than cacti, form a very large group. They are contained in about 30 plant families, 8 of which consist entirely of succulents, whilst in the others only a few succulents are found.

The more important of the families to which the succulent plants belong are: *Agavaceae*, *Liliaceae*, *Aizoaceae-Ficoideae*, *Asclepiadaceae*, *Crassulaceae*, *Euphorbiaceae*, *Compositae*, *Bromeliaceae*, and *Portulacaceae*.

AGAVACEAE

AGAVE (Plate 64). This genus contains over 300 species, which are native to America. They consist of shrubs or low bushes, having rosettes of elongated leaves possessing remarkable toughness. The margins of the leaves are toothed and usually have a strong spine at the tip. The leaves are greenish or bluish-green, often with a coloured margin. They are very attractive plants, but many are unsuitable for indoor cultivation, for they grow to large proportions. However, some of the smaller species make very good pot plants. Most make many offsets which usually root while still attached to the parent plant. These can be pulled off and propagated. In summer they prefer a very sunny position and grow well in a rich compost.

Agave Victoriae-Reginae (Plate 37). A very beautiful species, slow-growing. The leaves are numerous, 4 to 6 inches long, and about 2 inches broad. They are stiff and curved inwards; dull dark green, marked with oblique white lines. The terminal spines are long, and there may be 2 short spines near.

Agave Fernandi-Regis. Very similar to *A. Victoriae-Reginae*, with the upper side of leaves deeply concave and sharply keeled; the leaves are formed in rosettes without a stem. The inflorescence grows to quite a height. Flowers yellowish-green.

Agave felifera. The leaves form rosettes and are numerous and somewhat curved upwards; they are a shiny green with two or three white lines and a pale horny band, which becomes detached in thin filaments or threads. A straight spine forms the extreme tip of the leaf. This species is slow-growing and beautiful.

Agave stricta. This species forms spherical rosettes with the leaves very close. They are stiff and erect and slightly curved inwards; green, striped with pale grey, 14 inches in length. A very handsome species.

Agave americana (Plate 37). One of the larger Agaves, sometimes popularly called the "century plant". It derives its name from the supposition that it blooms but once in a century, but under favourable pot conditions this species has been made to flower in something like 20 years. To accomplish this an abundance of plant food and water must be given during the growing season. Small plants are attractive and can be grown all winter in the living-room, and, when the warm weather comes, can be placed out-of-doors. A large specimen will have 40 to 50 fleshy leaves arranged in a rosette, each leaf about 3 feet long and 3 inches broad, gradually tapering to a point tipped with a very sharp spine; the edges also have a few short spines. The leaves are a light glaucous green, but there are several varieties, some having a more or less broad yellow stripe down through the centre of the leaf, whilst in others the leaves are edged with yellow.

Other species to be recommended are: *A. Treleasei, A. Toumeyana, A. parviflora, A. Schotti, A. geminiflora.*

LILIACEAE

Although this family contains mostly bulbous plants, succulents are found in the following important genera: *Haworthia, Aloe, Astroloba, Bowiea,* and *Gasteria.*

HAWORTHIA. All Haworthias are miniature plants and well suited for window-sill collections, for they occupy little space and grow well in a compost of 1 part loam, 1 part coarse sand, and 3 parts leaf soil. The growing season is from March to October and during this period the plants should be frequently watered. In winter, watering should be reduced to an absolute minimum; in fact, it is even better to keep the soil on the dry side. All flower with long thin flexible racemes, single or branched, along which stand small white flowers with green or pink markings, always of the same type. The 6 free perianth leaves curve back at the tip, 3 remain erect, while 3 of them curve downwards. This is an invaluable characteristic and distinguishes the Haworthias from others of the family. They all come from South Africa.

Haworthia Chalwinii. A leafy-stemmed plant with the leaves in a rosette spiralled the whole

Plate 35. *Rhipsalis salicornioides*. P.91

Plate 36. *Lophophora Williamsii*. P.71

length of the stem. A particularly attractive species, dark green with whitish tubercles on the outer face of the leaves.

Haworthia Reinwardtii. Forms elongated rosettes. The leaves are triangular with a narrow base, dark green with numerous white tubercles arranged in regular transverse lines. A beautiful species.

Haworthia coarctata. The leaves form a spiral rosette the length of the stem, dark green, with small tubercles on raised longitudinal lines. The outside or back of the leaves is only sparsely covered with tubercles.

Haworthia attenuata. Has quite narrow, elongated leaves, with white tubercles in more or less broken transverse rows, more numerous on the outer face.

Haworthia fasciata. Similar to the preceding species. The rosettes are stemless, making many offsets. The leaves are numerous, up to $\frac{1}{2}$ inch broad and $1\frac{1}{2}$ inches long, rather shiny green with elongated pearly tubercles, which join together in transverse bands.

Haworthia limifolia. Forms rosettes, the leaves of which are about $1\frac{1}{2}$ inches long and $\frac{3}{4}$ inch broad at the base, lanceolate, and concave on the inner face. They are marked on both sides with 15 to 20 raised wavy transverse lines. The plant is dark green in colour.

Haworthia tessellata. Cape Province. The leaves are arranged in three series in stemless rosettes, and are 1 to $1\frac{1}{2}$ inches long, by about 1 inch broad, recurving from the base. The upper side of the leaf is almost transparent with darker transverse and longitudinal veins, the edges finely toothed. This species is one of the most charming varieties of the genus.

Haworthia margaritifera. The rosette is stemless, making many offsets, and growing up to about 6 inches in height. The leaves are lanceolate, dark green, both sides having large, roundish pearly tubercles.

Haworthia atrovirens. In its style of growth the plant very much resembles some species of *Sempervivum.* It forms a flat, dwarf rosette of small dark green toothed and pointed leaves; the lower surface of the leaf has also a row of thorny teeth in the centre.

ALOE (Plate 38). The genus includes both large and small species which have radial rosettes, but there are others which form a trunk or stem, either solitary or branched. There are about 200 species native to South Africa and the Mediterranean. The inflorescence grows from the leaf axils, simple or branched. The flowers grow in short-stalked racemes, and are numerous; red, yellow, or orange. The larger species are not suitable for the small collection, but the smaller species are valued as room and greenhouse plants. They require a rich, sandy compost, and good drainage. They are easily increased by cuttings or by offsets.

Aloe humilis. One of the most charming of the smaller species, forming a basal rosette, with pointed glaucous leaves, erect and curving inwards at the tips, covered on both sides with thorny spikes and toothed at the edges. The flowers are tubular, and bright red.

Aloe aristata. Cape Province. The plant is stemless with numerous leaves, grey-green, or green, with short white spines. The orange-red flowers appear in May to June. Requires a rich compost in which to grow. *A. longiaristata* is very similar.

Aloe brevifolia. Cape Province. A plant of more robust build, short-stemmed, with the rosettes of grey-green leaves very close together. The edges of the leaves are covered with whitish thorny teeth, a few of which are found on the upper and inner side of the leaves. The red flowers are held on a single strong but firmly erect pedicel.

Aloe ciliaris. Cape Province. The leaves of this species have a striped sheath and are recurved, linear-lanceolate and tapering, with toothed edges. The flowers are bright red, and appear in January to March.

Aloe ferox. Natal. The thick, broad and somewhat concave leaves are covered with very sharp thorny teeth on both sides as well as along the edges. The flower stalk is short, and carries a compact pyramid-shaped bunch of soft red flowers.

Aloe mitriformis. Grows taller and does not remain as a flat rosette. The stem can be seen between the leaves, which are thick, green, and spoon-shaped, with white, thorny, triangular teeth at the edges. The flowers are scarlet.

Aloe variegata (Plate 40). A very popular species, having beautiful markings caused by the white spots on the leaves being more or less arranged in stripes. The edges of the leaves are lined with minute closely set white teeth. The flowers are a beautiful red. It is well suited to conditions in the home and grows even better on a window-sill than in a green-house, for it enjoys the drier air. It should, however, be kept moist in summer, but given very little water in winter.

Other species to be recommended are: *A. Khamie-sensis* and *A. Krapouliana*.

ASTROLOBA. Closely related to the genus *Haworthia*, this genus was formerly known as *Apicra*. It includes about 12 species, and is a native of Cape Province. The plants are small and decorative, especially suitable for growing in the window-sill collection. They form leafy rosettes, stem-like and elongated. They require a compost consisting of 1 part loam, 1 part sharp sand, and 3 parts leaf-mould, the whole being well pressed around the roots. The growing season is from March to October, when they should receive water frequently.

Astroloba aspera. A small-growing species, with short leaves which are thick and covered on the outer and lower side with fine grey warts.

Astroloba pentagona. A very handsome species. The thick, fleshy green leaves are rigid, and pointed in shape. They are spirally arranged in five rows, one above the other around the stem, which is entirely hidden by them.

BOWIEA. There is only one species in the genus.

Bowiea volubilis. At first glance it looks very much like a green onion. It grows well in cultivation when planted with the bulb above the soil where it can be seen. It sends up one or two long, thin, bright green winding stems with many short, forking branches, more like the well-known asparagus plants. The greenish-white flowers are inconspicuous. It requires a very sandy but rich soil. When the stems begin to wither, watering should be gradually stopped and the bulb allowed to rest until it again shows signs of regrowth the following season.

GASTERIA. The plants in this genus have long or short, thick leaves, flat or triangular in section,

Plate 37. *Agave americana marginata*, the Century plant.
P.93
Agave Victoriae-Reginae. P.92

Plate 38. *Aloe* species. P.96

dagger or sword-shaped. Their colouring is light green to grey, and they are marked in every possible style or manner, some being smooth and some covered with rough tubercles. There are about 50 species. The flowers are red, green-edged, and more or less trumpet-shaped, flowering at almost any time. The plants are easy of cultivation if grown in half shade, and require frequent water in summer; during the winter they should be kept fairly dry. They are natives of South Africa.

Gasteria acinacifolia. The leaves form a rosette, sword-shaped and flattened on one side. They are a smooth, shining dark green with white dots.

Gasteria verrucosa. Probably the most handsome of the genus. Its concave green leaves are arranged one above the other in two series, running out to a point and curved upwards. They are entirely covered with small granular whitish-grey tubercles. If placed in a sunny spot in the winter season, the leaves assume shades of pink, and are very attractive.

Gasteria maculata. A very attractive species; the leaves are long and smooth, dark green, and splashed with round white spots which are more or less arranged to form bands across the leaves.

AIZOACEAE

The tribe Ficoideae in the family of Aizoaceae comprises about 120 genera, with several hundred species and varieties. They are better known as Mesembryanthemums (see Fig. 5, page 20), of which the greater number are natives of South Africa.

They are roughly divided into three categories: species with elongated stems, erect or prostrate; low-growing species; species that have been called "mimicry plants" because it has been observed how cleverly these plants match their surroundings in their native habitats.

They are found in regions notorious for long periods of drought, and in order to succeed in the struggle for life, the plants have been constructed to retain and hold moisture for as long as possible, and to protect themselves in various ways against excessive evaporation. This protection is achieved by:

(1) A reduction of the leaf surface resulting in a reduction in the number of stomata or breathing pores.

(2) A thickening of the epidermis or skin, so that the stomata lie deep below the surface.

(3) A covering of hairs or wax to prevent the stomata being dried up by the burning heat.

(4) The removal of the stomata to a part of the plant which is not exposed to the direct action of the sun's rays (mimicry plants).

Certain of the Ficoideae referred to as mimicry plants have a most remarkable structure of leaf tops which permits the light to penetrate down to the assimilating tissue, which would otherwise be deprived of all light, for in nature they grow buried in the soil, the upper surface only showing. Plants having these windowed leaves are found among the following genera: *Lithops*, *Fenestraria*, *Frithia*, and *Conophytum*.

APTENIA. Natives of the Cape Colony, these are small half shrubs which flower freely in summer and autumn, with reddish-purple flowers. The stems are prostrate, and bear fleshy leaves. Propagation is easy from seed and cuttings. They should be kept moderately dry in winter.

Aptenia cordifolia. A much-branched species, with prostrate stems. Var. *foliis variegatis* is similar, with the leaves beautifully marked with creamy white. Both varieties are very suitable for baskets.

ARGYRODERMA. The genus consists of mimicry forms. In their natural environment the plants can scarcely be distinguished among the broken stones and gravel in which they are found. They are of a whitish, grey-green colour, with no markings. They are natives of the Karroo and other parts of Africa. The growing period is in summer and they require a light position in the greenhouse or on the window-sill. Water should be given freely in summer, but they should be kept dry in winter. They are easily raised from seed.

Argyroderma octophyllum. A pretty plant with a smooth surface of a bluish-green colour and without markings. Flowers yellow, about $\frac{3}{4}$ inch in diameter. The plant is found in cultivation under the name of *A. testiculare.*

Argyroderma Schlechteri. The growths are usually solitary, consisting of one pair of leaves. The fissure is not wide open. The leaves are a white bluish-green with a smooth surface. Flowers, rosy red.

ARIDARIA. This genus forms branched shrubs, with fleshy leaves which are almost cylindrical. The flowers are very beautiful, white or yellowish-white. The growing period is in summer, when watering can be frequent, but in winter the plants should be kept on the dry side. There are about three species in the genus, the best of which is:

Aridaria splendens. Cape Province. This has cylindrical leaves, not united, bluntish, curved inwards, but recurving at the tips; they are pale green, with a few dark green tubercles, and a slightly frosted appearance. Flowers, yellowish-white.

BERGERANTHUS. These are stemless, very succulent plants. The leaves are long and generally pointed, forming rosettes. The flowers appear in June and July and are yellow. The growing period is in summer, and in winter the plants should be kept dry. They are easy to flower and easy to propagate from seed and cuttings. All are natives of Cape Province.

Bergeranthus multiceps. The species forms clumps of rosettes, with leaves 2 to 4 inches long. The flowers are yellow with a reddish tinge on the outside.

Bergeranthus scapiger. The leaves are long, 3 to 5 inches, and dark green. Flowers, golden-yellow, reddish on the outside. The plant is of larger proportion than *B. multiceps*.

Bergeranthus vespertinus. Intermediate between the two previous species. The leaves are erect at first, but later more or less prostrate, with a grey-green surface with some darker dots, and rather wrinkled. The flowers are yellow.

CARPOBROTUS. Natives of Cape Province, these are plants with prostrate branches. The leaves are large, 3 to 4 inches long, and triangular in section. The flowers are also large; red, yellow, yellowish-pink, or purple. They grow well in rich soil and propagate best from cuttings.

Carpobrotus acinaciforme. The leaves are about $3\frac{1}{2}$ inches long. The flower, about 5 inches in diameter, is a bright carmine-purple, opening at midday. Flowering season, July to November.

Carpobrotus edulis. The branches are angular, up

to 3 feet long, the leaves angled, with the keel finely toothed. The flowers, 3 to 4 inches in diameter, are yellow to pink or purple, opening at midday.

CHEIRIDOPSIS. These are very succulent plants of clustered growth, with 1 to 3 pairs of leaves per stem. They are natives of the Karroo desert. The growing period is chiefly from late summer to winter, and they require a light position and a moderate amount of water. They propagate easily from seed. During winter, the plants should be kept very dry. There are about 24 species.

Cheiridopsis candidissima. Probably the finest species in the genus. The whitish-grey leaves are long, boat-shaped, and almost erect, united from the base for about two-fifths of their length. In hot sunny weather, the leaves assume a white colour which is very attractive. The species flowers late in the season and requires careful treatment, especially with regard to watering.

Cheiridopsis cigarettifera. The leaves are about an inch long, jointed together during the resting period, when the young leaves are hidden in dry sheaths of the old leaves.

Cheiridopsis Meyeri. A peculiar plant. When growing, the white sheaths burst and a pair of leaves emerge which are united at their base. The leaves spread apart, and between them is developed a second pair united almost to the apex into a solid body and keeled over the top. They are pale grey-green in colour, with numerous darker dots. During the resting period they should be kept completely dry.

CONOPHYTUM. The genus is a most important one, for it contains some of the most interesting of the succulent plants. They are of dwarf habit, usually stemless, but some species form stems when old. The growths consist of small fleshy bodies which may be conical, spherical, ovate, or almost cylindrical, and are formed of two united leaves. In the centre of the upper part of the united leaves will be found a fissure, which may be very short or extend across the top. A solitary flower appears in this fissure on a stalk $\frac{1}{3}$ to 1 inch in length. The flowers may be white, yellow, pink, or violet. New bodies of Conophytums are formed within the old ones. They gradually withdraw the material from the old body till nothing remains but a dry skin, which encloses the young body and protects it during the dry period. Growth starts about August, when the plants require moisture. The period of growth lasts only for a few weeks, after which water must be restricted and the plants kept drier. In March, when the new bodies begin to form, some water can be given, but from May to August water should be entirely withheld, even if the bodies shrivel. The genus comprises over 200 species, all of which are extremely interesting.

Conophytum altile. Tufted plants, somewhat spherical, of a shining green, tinted purplish at the base, and marked on top with rather large dark green dots, those around the fissure at the edge of the surface almost forming a line.

Conophytum albescens. Stemless, and tufted. The bodies are laterally compressed or round, indented on top, pale grey-green indistinctly marked with large transparent dots, with the tips of the lobes tinged red. The flower is yellow.

Conophytum Batesii. Forms small tufts, the

Plate 39. *Ferocactus Wislizenii*. P.73

Plate 40. *Aloe variegata*. P.97

Plate 41. *Conophytum Tischeri*. P.106
Faucaria felina in flower. P.107

Plate 42. *Coryphantha aggregata.* P.84

bodies small, grey-green in colour and reddish at the base; the upper surface has a few dark dots.

Conophytum Braunsii. Forms short stems; the upper surface circular and slightly convex, outlined with a dark line. The flowers are violet.

Conophytum bilobum. A stemless plant, becoming branched and tufted when old. One of the larger species, pale grey-green in colour, with yellow flowers.

Conophytum concinnum. Forms clumps. The upper surface is usually circular, flat, and slightly convex, the bodies blue-green, and marked on the upper surface with darker dots.

Conophytum Elishae. Has blue-green bodies which grow to $1\frac{1}{2}$ inches long and terminate in a keeled cleft top. The species increases quickly and eventually forms an attractive clump. The flowers are bright yellow.

Conophytum ficiforme. Forms clumps of greyish-green bodies, often tinted with purple at the base, with conspicuous dark green dots on the top. The flower is bright pink and slightly scented.

Conophytum Meyerae. The bodies reach a height of 2 inches. The lobes are 1 inch long, with the inner side flat; the angles of the inner sides of the lobes are marked with a line of dots, and the surface is covered with small dark dots. Flowers, yellow.

Conophytum minutum. The clumps formed are roundish, greyish-green, without markings. The flowers are pale violet-red and produced regularly.

Conophytum Purpusii. Forms low clumps; the bodies are conical, bluish-grey-green, with the upper surface papillose and marked with small dark dots. Flowers, pale yellow.

Conophytum saxetanum. Forms clumps; the green

bodies numerous and close together, rounded above. The flowers are whitish.

Conophytum truncatellum. Forms clumps; the bodies are compressed, truncate, almost circular above, pale grey-green, with numerous small dots.

Conophytum Tischeri (Plate 41). Forms clumps; the bodies rounded, somewhat depressed above, the fissure surrounded by an irregular dark zone; grey-green with dark dots. Flowers, pale lilac.

Conophytum velutinum. The bodies are thick, ob-ovate, bluish-green, rather indistinctly sprinkled with dark green dots. Flowers, magenta.

DELOSPERMA. Plants of bushy habit, native to SW. Africa, they flower throughout the summer and often in winter. The leaves are short and swollen, triangular with a hook at the tip. They are light grey in colour, with very fine warts, or none at all. The small flowers have very short stems, and are whitish-yellow or red. All are easily grown and flower freely. They require a rich porous soil.

Delosperma echinatum. A free-flowering plant, with thick oval hemispherical leaves, pale green, and covered with papillae which are often tipped with a bristle. The flowers are solitary, whitish or yellowish. This is perhaps the best-known species.

Delosperma robustum. The greyish-green leaves are awl-shaped, blunt, with the inner side swollen at the base, and the back rounded and triangular at the tip. The flowers are lilac.

DINTERANTHUS. Natives of Great Namaqua-land, these are stemless plants, with the leaves very short and thick, united at the base. The upper side of the leaves is flat, the lower side rounded: they are whitish, without dots, or with numerous inconspicuous green dots. The flowers appear singly and are large and yellow in colour. The growing period is in summer, and they must be grown in a very light position. Even at this period water should be given very sparingly and in winter the plants should be kept quite dry.

Dinteranthus microspermus. Solitary, but branching when old. There are 1 to 2 pairs of leaves on a growth, and they are united for about half their length. Young plants are whitish to grey-green, with greenish dots. The flowers are yellow, with the petals tipped with red.

Dinteranthus Pole Evansii. The plants are solitary, with pairs of dove-grey leaves united half-way up; the flowers are glossy yellow. As with *D. microspermus*, water should always be given very sparingly.

FAUCARIA. These plants are found in the Karroo desert of South Africa. There are about 10 species that are popular with collectors. They are very succulent plants and all are of easy cultivation. The leaves are very crowded, united at the base, fleshy, keeled towards the tip, and have teeth along the edges. The growing period is in autumn and early winter. They require as much light as possible, and in autumn and winter should be watered freely. In summer, less water is required.

Faucaria albidens. The species has rosettes with 5 or 6 pairs of leaves 1 inch long, wider in the middle, elongated, triangular and tapering; they are fresh green with small dots, and the edges have 3 to 5 recurved teeth. The flower is golden-yellow.

Faucaria felina (Plate 41). The plant has keeled

and pointed leaves, indistinctly dotted with white, and with 3 to 5 recurved teeth at the edges. The flowers are golden-yellow.

Faucaria tigrina. A somewhat variable species, grey-green with numerous white dots in rows. The edges of the leaves have 9 to 10 stout teeth, which end in fine hairs. If kept in a light position the leaves become reddish. Flowers, golden-yellow.

Faucaria Brittenae. Surface grey-green, with distinct grey dots; edges of leaves and part of keel surrounded by whitish or reddish horny bands, with 3 or 4 hair-like teeth in the middle.

Faucaria tuberculosa. A very interesting species with very thick dark green leaves; the edges usually have 3 stout teeth and several undeveloped teeth. Flowers measure approximately 1½ inches, and are yellow.

FENESTRARIA. These much sought-after plants are natives of Namaqualand. The genus consists of 2 species of low-growing plants formed from a large number of erect club-shaped leaves, greenish-white in colour and having a distinct translucent "window". The plants in their natural environment are buried in the sand, and only the windowed tops of the leaves are to be seen. When grown under cultivation, and not under natural conditions, the plants should not be buried, for they are very liable to rot when the atmosphere contains much more moisture than in their native regions. The chief growing period is from early March throughout the summer months; during this period they should not be watered too frequently, and in winter they should be kept dry. Both species resent repotting, and if this is necessary great care should be exercised.

Fenestraria aurantiaca. The plants form cushions of many leaves, which are about an inch long. The leaves are not compressed into 1 or 2 lobes, but remain independent and form a rosette; they are club-shaped and gently curved upwards, with a convex top of a somewhat triangular shape. The window admits light to the heart of the plant, nature's adaptation so that sunlight can only penetrate to the chlorophyll by filtering through the "windows". The species produces orange-yellow flowers in August.

Fenestraria rhopalophylla. Very much like *F. aurantiaca*, except that the leaves are flatter at the top and shorter and more club-shaped. The flowers are white.

FRITHIA. This genus is a native of the West Transvaal. There is one species.

Frithia pulchra. A small stemless plant, with the leaves arranged in a rosette. These are almost cylindrical, and look as if they had been abruptly cut off, leaving a semi-transparent "window". The leaves are grey-green and the flower is carmine, white in the centre, and freely produced from June to August. It needs a warm, light position and the compost should be very sandy. In the early part of the year the plant should be kept dry, and in winter moderately moist. Easily grown from seed, flowering in the second year.

GIBBAEUM. Stemless plants with prostrate branches, the growths consist of ovate, obovate, or almost cylindrical bodies, which are slightly notched or distinctly divided into even or uneven lobes. The leaves are more or less united, but in some cases they are separated from each other above. The flower has a stalk and is white or rosy-lilac in colour. The growing period varies with the species. At all times they require to be grown in a light position. They are found in the Karroo, South Africa.

Gibbaeum album. The leaves are almost entirely joined together with a fissure at first hardly recognizable, but later opening. The leaves are whitish and covered with minute fine white hairs. The growing period is in summer, and during this period watering should not be too frequent. A beautiful species, having white flowers.

Gibbaeum pubescens. The leaves are united at the base, but of unequal length, the larger being $1\frac{1}{8}$ inches long, and the smaller about $\frac{1}{2}$ inch long; the surface is covered with felty hairs, giving a whitish-grey appearance. Violet-red flowers are produced in February or March. The period of growth is from December to March.

Gibbaeum velutinum. The pale bluish-green leaves are united at the base on prostrate branches. The flowers are white and produced in March to April. The growing period is December to June.

Gibbaeum Heathii. Forms clumps of bodies which are almost round, consisting of two round or oval equal leaves, united together for half their length. The surface is smooth and grass-green in colour. The white to creamish flower is produced in August and September.

GLOTTIPHYLLUM. Native to the Cape Province, this genus consists of easy to grow plants, with fleshy leaves crowded 4 or more to a growth

Plate 43. *Lithops* species, "living stones". P.111
Lithops pseudotruncatella with seed pods. P.113

Plate 44. *Pleiospilos Nelii* plants, with bud and flower. P.116

and all tongue-shaped. The flowers are very large, and glossy yellow. The growing period lasts from June to the end of January. The compost should not be too rich and should consist of 1 part loam, a half part leaf soil, and 1 part sand.

Glottiphyllum depressum. The leaves are very crowded, with 3 or 4 pairs to a growth, and arranged in two rows. The flowers are yellow.

Glottiphyllum linguiforme. A fast-growing plant. The fresh glossy green leaves are arranged in two rows and tongue-shaped, about $2\frac{1}{4}$ inches long and $1\frac{1}{2}$ inches broad. The flowers are large and golden-yellow.

LITHOPS (Plate 43). These are probably the most sought after of succulent plants. They comprise one, two, or more growths, in clumps, each growth consisting of a conical or almost cylindrical pair of leaves, almost completely united, divided only by a fissure across the upper surface. They are endemic to Namaqualand and the Karroo. So closely do they resemble stones that they are often referred to by the descriptive name of "living stones". They grow in nature in very dry desert regions, partly buried in the sand. The growing period is from March to September. At all times they should be kept in a light position, and planted in a compost which is very sandy, and the bodies should not be buried in the soil up to the upper surface but should project well above. Propagation is best from seed, but cuttings can be successfully rooted. They can be divided into two sections; those which have an opaque "window" and those which have an entirely or partly translucent "window". The species have an infinite variation in the pattern of the delicate markings. No two plants seem to be alike in this respect, but they have been classified into 70 distinct species.

Lithops alpina. The bodies are small, with the upper surface slightly convex, pale brown, with fine brown markings, and freely dotted. Flower, yellow.

Lithops aurantiaca. Forms clumps, rounded on the top, with a shallow fissure. The body is brown, the flowers orange-yellow.

Lithops bella. Grows in clumps, with 1 to 6 brownish-yellow bodies, which are slightly rounded at the top. A very beautiful plant with pure white flowers.

Lithops Comptonii. A lovely small "windowed" plant, forming clumps. The fissures are deep. The body is olive-green, the flower yellow.

Lithops Framesi. This is a clump-forming plant. The sides of the body are reddish-grey, with a dark grey "window" and a few scattered grey markings.

Lithops Fulleri. The bodies are dove-grey, their upper surface with pitted markings which consist of brownish branched lines. The outer edge often has brownish-red dots. Flower, white.

Lithops karasmontana. A very popular species, grey to bluish-yellow, the upper surface pitted and wrinkled, usually brownish to ochre coloured. Having a thick epidermis, the old leaves persist a long time. Flower, white.

Lithops lateritia. Forms clumps. It is rusty red with a few markings, the upper surface being greyish, with a fairly deep fissure. Flower, white.

Lithops Lesliei. One of the best of the Lithops,

Flower of *Stapelia variegata*.
P. 122

Plate 45. *Stapelia* flower with horsefly.
P. 121

Plate 46. *Crassula grisea.* P.125
Cotyledon orbiculata. P.128

forming 1 or 2 bodies. It is coffee-coloured, the upper surface pitted with a network of dark greenish-brown markings. Flower, golden-yellow.

Lithops olivacea. A beautiful plant, forming small clusters, with green "windows", often flecked whitish. The body of the plant is olive-green. Flowers, yellow.

Lithops Peersii. A popular Lithops, forming clumps; the bodies are ochre or greenish, upper surface flat, with dark grey dots; the edge of the upper surface and the fissure are a lighter colour. Flower, glossy yellow.

Lithops umdausensis. The bodies are olive-green to brown with blue-green markings in the form of branching lines, the fissures running right across the top of the bodies. Flower, white.

Lithops pseudotruncatella (Plate 43). A very free-growing species, forming clumps. The upper surface is roundish, the bodies pale brownish-grey, with a network of veins and dots on the upper surface, like a piece of finely veined marble. Flowers, golden-yellow.

Lithops turbiniformis. The species has a wrinkled top of light rusty brown with darker brown in the furrows, the fissure running right across. The bodies are grey. Flower, yellow.

LAMPRANTHUS. These bushy plants are either erect, spreading, or prostrate. They are fast growing, and propagate easily from cuttings. They are native to Cape Province.

Lampranthus aureus. This species grows 12 to 16 inches high, and has golden-yellow flowers 2 inches in diameter.

Lampranthus blandus. A very showy plant, with pink flowers, 2 inches in diameter.

Lampranthus coccineus. A larger plant with scarlet flowers.

Lampranthus spectabilis. A prostrate plant, with purple-red flowers, 2 inches in diameter.

NANANTHUS. The genus includes about a dozen species of small, compact plants, the growths having 4 to 6 pairs of leaves. They are native to South Africa. The growing period is in the summer, the plants requiring a position in full light. As the root stocks are long, they should be accommodated in tall pots, in a very sandy compost.

Nananthus rubrolineatus. A very interesting species forming clumps which are more or less prostrate. The flowers are yellow, the petals having a very distinct line down the middle.

Nananthus vittatus. The leaves are of different lengths; narrow, triangular, and rough. Flowers, pale yellow, the petals having a fine red middle line.

OPHTHALMOPHYLLUM. The dwarf, stemless plants resemble *Lithops*, the bodies consisting of a pair of united leaves, translucent over their whole surface. The flowers are white, pink, or lilac. The chief growing period is from September to February, and the plants require a very light position. Great care must be exercised in the watering of these plants. The compost should be very sandy, for they dislike stagnant moisture. There are about 15 species.

Ophthalmophyllum Friedrichiae. The growths are usually solitary, the fissure running right across the top, gaping, and about ¼ inch deep. The body is green, but takes on a copper-red colour during the resting period. The top of the plant has a very transparent "window", with large pale dots along the lower edge. The flowers are white.

Ophthalmophyllum Maughanii. This species usually has only one body, pale green in colour, with pale yellowish-green "windows", which are almost transparent. It is one of the largest species, and has white flowers.

OSCULARIA. The plants in this genus are easy to grow and very free flowering. The growing period is spring and summer. They propagate easily from seed and from cuttings. They are shrubs with erect or spreading branches, of a pleasing blue-green or grey-green colour, and have attractive pink flowers in spring.

Oscularia caulescens. Forms a spreading bush. The leaves are ¾ inch long, and have 2 to 3 small reddish teeth on the edges towards the tip. The flowers are scented and pink in colour.

Oscularia deltoides. There are several varieties of this species, all of which branch freely, forming dense plants.

PLEIOSPILOS. Comprising about 30 species, this genus is much sought after by collectors. In their shape and colouring the plants closely resemble pieces of granite. The growing period lasts from August to December, during which time moderate amounts of water should be given. During the remainder of the year the plants should be kept completely dry. They require a position in full light, and the compost should be very sandy. Propagation is easy from seed, many of the seedlings flowering in their first year. There are about 15 recognized species.

Pleiospilos Bolusii. A dark, grey-green plant, split into equal halves, sometimes growing to 4 inches in size. The surface is smooth, the chin-like portion usually rather warty. The flowers are golden-yellow, sometimes 3 inches across, and last for a few days.

Pleiospilos magnipunctatus. The growths have 2 to 4 leaves which are very thick and taper abruptly; they are grey-green with numerous green dots. Flowers, yellow.

Pleiospilos Nelii (Plate 44). A plant very similar in appearance to *P. Bolusii*, but more smoothly rounded and more hemispherical in appearance. The fissure is deep. The flowers have bronzy petals, shading to white at the base, and dark-coloured anthers.

Pleiospilos simulans. Can easily be distinguished from *P. Nelii* by the much fatter leaves, which have practically no keels and are, as a rule, much greyer in colour, with more clearly marked dots. The flowers may be yellow, pale yellow, or even orange.

RHOMBOPHYLLUM. This is a genus of tufted succulent plants with fleshy roots. The leaves are united at the base, and are not unlike the leaves of the *Faucaria*. They are keeled above, the lower side being drawn forward like a chin, and have rather distinct white edges, with 1 or 2 short teeth. The surface is smooth and green with whitish dots. From 3 to 7 golden-yellow flowers grow on a stalk. Three species are recognized, all of which are easy growing and free flowering. The growing period is from June to November and they require a sunny position. Even in the growing period watering should not be too frequent.

Rhombophyllum rhomboideum. A popular plant in collections, stemless and forming clumps. The leaf rosettes lie close to the ground with 8 to 10 leaves. Flowers, golden-yellow, reddish outside.

STOMATIUM. The young plants are stemless, but they have short stems when old. They are tufted plants forming clumps, the leaves 4 to 6 on a growth. The genus is a native of Cape Province. The growing period is in summer, when they require a light position. In winter, they should be kept dry. All are easy to grow.

Stomatium erminium. The leaves are close together and spreading, with a narrow base, the upper side flat, the lower side convex and keeled; the edges have 3 or 4 short, straight teeth. The plant is grey-green in colour, and the leaves are roughened with numerous rays of transparent dots. Flower, yellow.

Stomatium suaveolens. Has very fleshy leaves, erect or spreading, with the backs very rounded and distinctly keeled towards the tip; the edges have 1 to 5 small teeth; pale green, with pale dots. Flower, yellow.

TITANOPSIS. These are very interesting plants, stemless, and forming clumps. They have very fleshy roots. The growths form rosettes of 6 to 8 glaucous green to purplish leaves, covered with roundish warts. The flowers are yellow or orange. The growing period is in summer and all species require as much light as possible. Water can be given frequently in summer, but they should be kept dry in winter. They are easily propagated from seed.

117

The compost should be very sandy. The genus is native to S. Africa and Great Namaqualand.

Titanopsis calcarea. An interesting species, the leaves having the appearance of pieces of limestone. It forms rosettes of grey-green to purple leaves with whitish or rosy warts towards their broadened tips. Great care should be exercised to see that no water lodges between the leaves, for these will rot. The flowers are orange, and produced on short stalks.

Titanopsis Fulleri. A beautiful plant with rosettes formed of 5 or 6 pairs of leaves, which terminate in a roundish triangular tip; the backs of the leaves are roundly keeled, the upper surface flat and slightly concave. The leaves are a beautiful blue-green with a reddish tinge, the surface covered with dark dots. This wart-like roughness can vary in colour from almost pure white to purple. Flower, yellow.

Titanopsis setifera. This is a distinctive species, having leaves thicker and greener than the others in the genus. The little warts are not so prominent, but small teeth protrude on the edges, and also a few on the upper and under surfaces.

TRICHODIADEMA. Native to Cape Province, this genus comprises about 7 species. The plants are bushy and of tufted habit. All are easy to grow and flower freely. They grow throughout the year, but should be given a short resting period in January and February. They enjoy a sunny position and can be freely watered, except during the resting period.

Trichodiadema densum. Has semicircular, fleshy, elongated leaves. The flowers are carmine-violet, and are produced early in the year and again late in the year.

Plate 47. *Mammillaria microcarpa.* P.87

Plate 48. *Cotyledon undulata.* P.129

ASCLEPIADACEAE

CARALLUMA. Native to S. and N. Africa, and Abyssinia, this genus comprises a large number of species of succulent shrubs with 4- to 6-angled stems. Cultivation should be as described under *Stapelia.* The flowers are generally in groups and vary in size, with 5 deep lobes. They are variously coloured and marked, and evil-smelling.

Caralluma burchardii. A native of the Canary Islands. The plant forms clumps, with olive-green or grey-green stems about 10 inches high, 4-angled, with erect teeth. The flowers are small, produced in groups at the ends of the stems, and have a brown corolla with white hair.

Caralluma europaea. A native of the Mediterranean countries. It has quaint squarish 4-angled stems, greyish-green with a few indistinct reddish markings. The flowers are ½ inch in diameter, in groups of 5 to 8 at the top of the stems, yellow, with purple bands, and hairy towards the centre.

CEROPEGIA. These plants are found in tropical and southern Africa. Their fleshy stems may be leafy or without leaves. The twining species are pretty plants with tuberous roots. The flowers are strangely shaped, resembling lanterns, and are of various designs and colourings.

Ceropegia juncea. A fast-growing climber, its leaves are small, scale-like, arranged in pairs, and stand straight out from the stem. The flowers are green, with purplish-brown spots, and grow together at the top.

Ceropegia stapeliaeformis. Cape Province. The stems, about ½ inch thick, are dull green, marbled with dark green, brown, and white. The flowers are very delicate in form and colour, and are erect, appearing in groups, and blooming for several days; the corolla is about 2 inches long and not joined together at the top, the tips turning outwards, and is dark brown with white inside. The young branches are thin and twiny, with barely visible leaves.

Ceropegia Woodii. A pretty plant and very attractive when climbing on a miniature trellis. The stems are slender, forming small tubers at the nodes, the leaves stalked and heart-shaped, dark green marbled with white. Flower, pinky-brown.

DUVALIA. Native to SW. Africa and S. Africa, this genus consists of small plants with prostrate stems forming clumps. The stems are 4- to 6-angled, short and thick, with short teeth. The flowers are solitary, or grow several together, like small stars. Cultivation is as for *Stapelia.* About 15 species are classified.

Duvalia elegans. Cape Province. The stems are prostrate, about $1\frac{1}{2}$ inches long and $\frac{1}{2}$ inch thick; the angles blunt and toothed. Flowers are blackish-violet inside, with long purple hairs.

ECHIDNOPSIS. This genus consists of 10 species, the plants having 6 to 10 spineless tubercled angles, and terminating in a rudimentary leaf. The flowers are small, and appear near the top in clusters. The plants are natives of NE. Africa.

Echidnopsis cereiformis. Eritrea. Has dull green stems about 12 inches long and 1 inch thick, 8-angled. The flowers are brownish outside, bright yellow inside. Growing period, summer to autumn.

Aeonium arboreum. P. 130

Plate 49. *Aeonium* species. P. 129

Plate 50. *Aeonium domesticum variegatum.* P.130

Plate 51. *Sedum* species. P.132

Plate 52. *Sedum Morganianum*, Burro's tail. P.135

Echidnopsis dammanniana. Eritrea. The stems are about 8 inches long, ¾ inch thick, 8- to 10-angled. The purplish-brown flower is yellow at the centre.

HEURNIA. Found in S. and E. Africa and Eritrea, this genus consists of nearly 50 species including many delightful plants, all with short stems, usually 4- to 6-angled, and more or less toothed. The fleshy flowers, variously coloured and marked, smell slightly of carrion. Heurnias are distinguished from the Stapelias by having the 5 lobes of the flower supplemented by 5 smaller lobes or points, the latter appearing between the main corolla lobes. Cultivation is as for *Stapelia*, but great care should be exercised when watering, especially in winter.

Heurnia Pillansii. Has 20- to 24-angled stems, covered with tubercles ending in fine hairs. The flower is bell-shaped, with elongated lobes, yellow, with crimson flecks inside. The plant is liable to rot if moisture is excessive.

Heurnia primulina. The 4- to 5-angled stems are pale green, with reddish markings. Flower waxy, creamy-white, with reddish markings, round a purple-black inner corolla. This is a very beautiful plant.

STAPELIA (Plate 45). The genus includes about 99 species. They carry remarkable flowers which have carrion odours. They are endemic to semi-arid regions from India to S. Africa. The Stapelias are plants of low growth, with soft, square leafless stems, the edges of which bear fleshy tooth-like points, representing the rudiments of leaves. The teeth are fixed in alternate pairs, two at opposite angles, and then two higher up at the other angles. The flowers appear on short stems bearing 1 to 4 flowers at the base of the youngest shoots. In many cases they overhang the pots in which the plants are grown. The petals are yellowish or dark brown, plain-coloured or marked with darker spots, and mostly wrinkled or grooved. Many species are suitable for growing in the window-sill. In summer, they require plenty of air, and during this growing period they should be kept moist by frequent spraying on warm days. They require a compost of 2 parts loam, 2 parts leaf soil, 3 parts sharp sand, and 1 part broken brick, and should be repotted every year.

Stapelia variegata (Plate 45). Often found in collections, and may be taken as the type plant of the smaller species, with medium-sized flowers. Stems 4 inches high, glaucous green, but when kept in a sunny position they sometimes turn reddish. Flowers, up to 5 in number, develop from the base of the new stems. They are 2 inches or more in diameter, swollen in a circular ring round the central part, yellowish ochre marbled with purple, and without hair.

Stapelia nobilis. Transvaal. Has pale green stems with a velvety appearance, 6 to 10 inches long, and about 1¼ inches diameter, with small erect teeth. The flower is very large, star-shaped, up to 8 inches in diameter, with a somewhat bell-shaped tube at the centre.

Stapelia grandiflora. The stems are more or less club-shaped and pale green, 10 to 12 inches long and 1½ inches thick. The flowers, produced from the same centre, number 3 to 10, and have a diameter of about 6 inches; they have dark purple-brown petals covered with soft, shiny, reddish-brown

Plate 53. *Dudleya farinosa.* P.136

Plate 54. *Epiphyllum* hybrid (Orchid Cactus). P.89

hairs, the margins being edged with long, silvery hairs. The carrion scent in this species is only faintly noticeable.

CRASSULACEAE

In this family there are nearly 1,000 species, belonging to 25 genera, and these are grouped into 6 sub-families: namely, Crassuloideae, Kalanchoideae, Cotyledonoideae, Sempervivoideae, Sedoideae, and Echeverioideae.

Sub-Family CRASSULOIDEAE

These are succulent shrubs forming clumps with fleshy leaves arranged opposite one another, often crowded into rosettes, but in other plants well apart. The flowers are fairly small, white or pink; the petals and the stamens are the same in number, usually 5 of each.

CRASSULA. Most species in this genus are natives of S. Africa. There are considerably over 200 species. A few are annuals, and because of the diversity of shape and form, they can be a source of interest for anyone making a collection of them.

SHRUBBY SPECIES:

Crassula arborescens. Cape Province. Of shrubby habit with thick fleshy stem and branches. The leaves are wide at the base, roundish, obovate, fleshy, and are grey-green, often with a red margin and reddish spots on the upper surface. The flowers appear in clusters, pink or white, and later red. This species is easy to cultivate. Growing season, March to September.

Crassula argentea. Cape Province. A succulent shrub with a thick stem and stout branches, reaching a height in its native land of 10 feet. The leaves are oval, shining green; the flowers pale pink.

Crassula falcata. Cape Province. A beautiful plant, growing to a height of 3 feet. The thick, grey leaves have a sharp edge resembling a sickle in contour, and are fixed along the straight stem in such a way that 2 rows turn to the right and 2 rows to the left, giving the plant a two-sided flat appearance. The lovely flowers appear in summer, as much-branched clusters of false umbels, brilliant red in colour.

Crassula rotundifolia. A similar plant to *C. falcata,* but the fleshy green leaves are almost round and very flat, thinning out at the edges, with a soft coat of velvet; they are obliquely attached to the stem in a similar way to those of *C. falcata.*

Crassula lactea. A semi-shrub, with dark green leaves and white flowers, the latter produced in midwinter. Makes a fine pot plant if given a rich sandy compost. Easy to grow.

Crassula lycopodioides. Cape Province. A small, bushy plant whose thin branches are completely covered with 4 rows of closely packed leaves. The minute flowers, yellowish-white, are almost sessile, and spring from the axils of the leaves in the upper portions of the stem. Easy to grow and easy to propagate, by cuttings.

Crassula perfoliata. Cape Province. A semi-shrub, very similar in appearance to *C. falcata.* The stems are erect and fleshy, with leaves 3 to 4 inches long, tapering, and concave above. The flower is scarlet.

Crassula rupestris. Cape Province. A beautiful

plant forming a prostrate bush. The fleshy, round-ish or oval leaves are grey-green in colour with brown dots and a brown margin. The flowers are attractive. A very useful plant for baskets.

LOW-GROWING SPECIES

Crassula alstonii. Namaqualand. Has thick, smooth, compact and incurved leaves, forming a grey, almost white, plant. The flowers are small and white. This species requires full light and should be rested in summer. Growing period, October and November. Compost should consist of 2 parts leaf soil, 1 part loam, 2 parts sand.

Crassula columnaris. Namaqualand. An interest-ing plant, grey in colour, with the leaves about an inch across in 4 close rows. The flowers, white or yellowish-orange, appear October and November. Requires similar treatment to *C. alstonii.*

Crassula Cooperi. Cape Province. A dense, low-growing plant, 3 to 4 inches high, the leaves forming a rosette of green leaves with darker markings. The flower is flesh-coloured. Attractive, and easy to flower.

Crassula deceptrix. Namaqualand. A beautiful, low-growing plant, its short, angular leaves tightly pressed together to form a small column. The white flowers appear in October and November. This species should be rested in summer. The growing period is in winter.

Crassula grisea (Plate 46). A fine species with long, narrow leaves. In course of time the plant forms clumps. The largest leaves are at the base, while the leaves higher up develop small branches out of their axils. The leaves, arranged in opposite pairs, are oblong to oblong lanceolate, and covered with numerous fine papillae, so that they have a greenish-grey appearance; they are sometimes red at the margins. The flowers are white and small. This plant is easy to grow. It likes sun and warmth, but at no time should it have too much water.

Crassula Justus Corderoy. A slow-growing species, with green leaves flecked with brown, the whole surface covered with short white hairs. The reddish flowers are produced in midsummer.

Sub-Family KALANCHOIDEAE

This consists of a large group of plants, with three divisions, *Bryophyllum*, *Kalanchoe*, and *Kitchingia*, all having tubular flowers in four parts with the petals united, except at the tips.

KALANCHOE. These plants form shrubs, and grow erect. They are natives of Asia, Africa, and America. Some species are suitable for growing in rooms. All require a compost consisting of 2 parts leaf soil, 1 part loam, and 1 part sharp sand. The growing period is in summer.

Kalanchoe beharensis. A tree-like plant, with plush-like leaves, silvery on the underside, green and rust-coloured on the top. The species sheds the lower leaves, leaving only a few pairs at the top of the plant. Flowers are hardly ever produced in cultivation.

Kalanchoe Daigremontianum. More popularly known as *Bryophyllum Daigremontianum.* An erect-growing plant, becoming about 36 inches high. The shiny green leaves, 5 inches long, are irregularly flecked on the underside. The edges are crenulate, with adventitious buds growing in the notches.

Flowers, yellow to pink. The adventitious buds, taken from the leaves and placed upon soil, soon grow into attractive young specimens.

Kalanchoe tomentosa. A lovely species, with branched stems. The leaves are obovate, elongated, the surface covered all over with short hairs. They are yellowish-white, the upper part having brown pointed crenulations.

Kalanchoe marmorata. A shrubby plant, branching from the base. The green leaves have a grey waxy coating, both sides being mottled with large brown markings. The flower is white. A very beautiful species.

Kalanchoe Blossfeldiana. A small shrub with erect stems, about 12 inches high. The leaves are dark green, edged with red. The scarlet flower appears from January to April. Makes a very beautiful flowering plant.

Kalanchoe tubiflorum. More commonly known as *Bryophyllum tubiflorum.* The stems are erect, about 20 inches high, the leaves almost cylindrical, often slightly grooved, and crenulate, with adventitious buds growing towards the tips. Flower, orange-red.

Sub-Family COTYLEDONOIDEAE

This comprises three principal genera: namely, *Adromischus*, *Cotyledon*, and *Umbilicus*, and can be identified by the fact that it has the number of stamens equal to twice that of the petals.

ADROMISCHUS. There are about 20 species which are fairly common in collections, for they are easy to grow. Although the flowers are not as beautiful as the Cotyledons, the leaves are most attractive. They are natives of Namaqualand and the Cape

Province. They should be grown in a compost consisting of 3 parts loam, 3 parts leaf-mould, 3 parts sharp sand, 1 part broken brick, and 1 part mortar rubble.

Adromischus festivus. A fascinating plant; the leaves are so coloured as to remind one of plover's eggs, grey-green with darker markings.

Adromischus Cooperi. Very similar to *A. festivus*, grey-green in colour, usually with darker markings. The leaves narrow towards the base, and are more thickened towards the top of the plant.

Adromischus maculatus. Has flat, grey-green leaves, spotted reddish-brown on both sides. The leaves have a short point at the top and are slightly rough at the edges. This is probably the best known species.

Adromischus mamillaris. A low-growing plant. The leaves, green flecked with brown, are semi-circular in cross section, narrowed each side, about $1\frac{1}{2}$ inches long, $\frac{1}{2}$ inch wide. They are grooved on the upper surface with definite margins.

COTYLEDON. The genus comprises some lovely plants, distinguished from the Crassulas by their five-sectioned bell-shaped flowers. Included in this genus are small and large plants, branched, with fleshy leaves of a variety of shapes. They are easy to grow, but require a light position. The compost should consist of 4 parts loam, 1 part sharp sand, with some broken bricks and old mortar rubble. They can be freely watered in summer, but only occasionally in winter. The plants are natives of S. Africa.

Cotyledon orbiculata (Plate 46). Cape Province. Makes a lovely plant, owing to its leaves being

Plate 55. *Echeveria* species. P.137

Plate 56. *Echeveria Derenbergii.* P.137

heavily powdered, white, with a delicate edging of carmine or pink. They are flat, obovate, with a short point, and arranged in opposite pairs on a rather woody stem. The long flower stalk terminates in an umbel of pendent reddish or yellow flowers.

Cotyledon undulata (Plate 48). A very beautiful succulent plant with fleshy, flat, wing-shaped leaves, rounded at the top, with a wavy edge, and thickly covered over the whole surface with a white powder. The flowers appear on a graceful stock in a pendent umbel, and are bell-shaped, yellowish-red, and marked with a few delicate red stripes.

UMBILICUS. The genus, of Mediterranean origin, comprises low plants with tuberous roots. It is only occasionally cultivated in this country. After flowering, the plant should be kept quite dry. It grows best in a rich compost.

Umbilicus pendulinus. The leaves are long-stalked, circular, and green with reddish streaks. The pendent flowers are yellowish-white and grow on a stem about 16 inches high.

Sub-Family SEMPERVIVOIDEAE

This group includes the genera *Aeonium, Greenovia, Sempervivum, Aichryson,* and *Monanthes.*

AEONIUM (Plates 49, 50). Natives of the Canary Islands, Madeira, and N. Africa, these plants form rosettes of leaves at the ends of stems of branches. There are about 36 species and many hybrid forms. They are easy to grow, very suitable for cultivation in living-rooms, and should be freely watered in summer. The compost recommended is 2 parts leaf soil, 1 part loam, and 1 part sharp sand.

Aeonium arboreum (Plate 49). Grows to a height of 3 feet. The robust stem, or trunk, terminates in a flat rosette of elongated, tightly compressed green leaves 3 to 4 inches in length and about ¾ inch broad, with white hairs along the edges. The flower stalk forms a long truss of golden-yellow flowers which appear in spring.

Aeonium arboreum atropurpureum. A purple-leafed form commonly met with in collections.

Aeonium caespitosum. A low-growing leafy plant with short stems and branches. The leaves, which are green with reddish stripes and have many white hairs along the edges, form dense rosettes. Requires as much sun as possible.

Aeonium domesticum (Plate 50). The best-known species, especially in the variegated form. The rosettes are loosely formed, the flower yellow.

Aeonium sedifolium. Canary Islands. A small species, 4 to 6 inches high, with woody stems and branches. The reddish-brown leaves are compressed into rosettes at the ends of the branches. Flowers, yellow.

Aeonium tabulaeforme. An interesting plant with sessile plate-like rosettes, the leaves grass-green. The plant flowers when 2 to 3 years old and dies after flowering. Propagation is easy from seed, and it is possible to propagate from leaves. The most suitable are medium-sized leaves pulled off and placed in a sandy compost.

GREENOVIA. The genus is a small one consisting of 4 species, natives of the Canary Islands. They are of easy cultivation, especially suitable for growing in window-sills. The plants require a rich but

Plate 57. *Carnegiea gigantea*. P.59

Plate 58. *Euphorbia meloformis* in flower. P.140

sandy compost, with a few chippings of limestone added. The leaves form rosettes which die after flowering. Bright yellow flowers are produced in April and May. Plenty of water should be given in the growing season, but the plants should be kept fairly dry in winter.

Greenovia aurea. Forms low clumps. The cup-shaped rosettes are grey-green, covered with a blue-green waxy coating. A beautiful species.

Greenovia gracilis. Forms clumps, somewhat prostrate. The rosettes are numerous and small, bright grey-green, with a covering of whitish wax.

SEMPERVIVUM. The genus consists of plants which are hardy in England, though native to the European Alps. The species form clumps and are often seen growing in rock gardens, but when planted in pans they make interesting additions to the succulent plant collection. Species hybridize easily and there are many forms. The number of distinct species has been reduced to about 30.

Sempervivum arachnoideum. A beautiful plant, commonly known as the "cobweb plant" because of the very fine hairs spun like a cobweb between the tips of the leaves. Flowers, carmine. There are a number of varieties differing from one another by the size of the rosettes. The growing period is in summer. The rosettes die after flowering.

Other species to be recommended are: *S. Allionii, S. calcareum, S. Funckii, S. soboliferum, S. tectorum.*

MONANTHES. There are several species, which have small dense rosettes of leaves, and the plants form neat little cushions.

Monanthes laxiflora. An interesting small plant

with many leafy stems. The leaves are thick and the flowers vary from yellow to purplish. The growing season is in summer, when watering should be frequent. In winter, plants should be kept on the dry side.

Sub-Family SEDOIDEAE

In this sub-family, the most important and interesting plants are to be found in the genus *Sedum*.

SEDUM (Plates 51, 52). There are approximately 500 species, endemic to the European Alps, Asia, Japan, Africa, and the Americas, and varying from compact to shrubby forms. Many are hardy in Britain. It is the non-hardy plants, however, that are usually grown in indoor collections. They make ideal beginner's plants, growing in full light and sun. A good all-round compost consists of 4 parts loam, 1 part each of sharp sand, broken brick, and old mortar rubble. They should be frequently watered in summer and about every 2 or 3 weeks in winter.

Sedum dendroideum. Mexico. Grows to quite a large bush, with shiny green leaves and showy yellow flowers.

Sedum pachyphyllum. Mexico. A small shrub-like plant with club-shaped leaves, greyish-green with a lighty waxy covering, and with a reddish tinge at the ends. The flowers are yellow, and arise in a compact bunch.

Sedum Palmeri. Mexico. Forms rosettes on the ends of the branches. The leaves are grey-green with rounded tips, the flower orange-yellow.

Sedum Stahlii. Mexico. A very beautiful plant, with oval leaves dark green to brownish-red. The numerous slender stems, intricately branched, are more or less prostrate at the base of the plant. It is easily propagated from leaf cuttings.

Sedum Treleasei. Mexico. Thick leaves, curved somewhat upwards, pale green, with a delicate blue-grey covering. The pale yellow flowers are united in an erect umbel.

Sedum Adolphi. Mexico. Forms a small shrub, with fleshy leaves and branches. The leaves are alternate, more crowded towards the tip, yellowish-green with reddish edges. The white flowers appear in March and April.

Sedum dasyphyllum. A small tufted evergreen perennial from Europe and N. Africa. It has, however, become firmly naturalized on old walls in various parts of southern England. Easily recognized by its tiny growth, egg-shaped and very fleshy pinkish-grey leaves arranged in opposite pairs, and its dainty small pinkish flowers on two branched free-flowering cymes. The plant much dislikes moisture, but is very easy to grow. There are three varieties, all of which are nearly hardy.

Sedum kamtschaticum. NE. Asia. A glabrous plant with a stoutish root stock from which many-branched shoots spring. The shoots end in leafy cymes of large, rich, orange-yellow flowers, which appear from June to September. It rarely exceeds 6 inches in height.

Sedum lineare. China and Japan. A rather straggly glabrous evergreen species. There is a stronger growing form, *S. lineare robustum*, with grey-green instead of bright green leaves, and paler coloured flowers; also a pretty form, *S. lineare variegatum*, which has a margin of white surrounding the narrow leaves, pink stems, and is robust in growth. The latter variety is often met with under the name *S. sarmentosum*.

Sedum Sieboldii. Japan. A very lovely plant, often used in hanging baskets. It has carrot-like tubers, and dies back in winter. In late spring it sends up lengthening shoots with roundish stemless leaves in threes. These shoots terminate in flat umbels of rosy-purple flowers, which are very attractive against the glaucous leaves. A variegated variety is perhaps the more popular. It differs from the type in having a large area of chrome yellow in the middle of each of its blue-grey leaves.

Sedum spathulifolium. Although this plant is quite hardy, it is very attractive when grown in a pan. A native of western N. America, it is evergreen, glaucous, forming close mats composed of flattish, fleshy-leafed rosettes. If grown in a sunny spot, the leaves become tinged with red. In May and June, yellow flowers appear which are half an inch in diameter. The variety *Cassa Blanca* makes a very attractive little plant, rather more miniature than the type, but with the rosettes so heavily covered with a whitish farina as to cover completely the glaucous or red colouring.

Sedum Chaneti. China. A very striking plant. Forms rosettes of fleshy, glaucous, spine-tipped leaves, the rosettes being of varying sizes. On full-sized ones, ascending spires burst into dense little pyramids of white blooms, with deep purple anthers. Flowering period, September and October.

Sedum altissimum. S. Europe and N. America. A very distinct species with a strong alpine-growing habit. The many-branching stems are thickly set

Plate 59. *Euphorbia mammillaris*. P. 141

Euphorbia ingens. P. 141

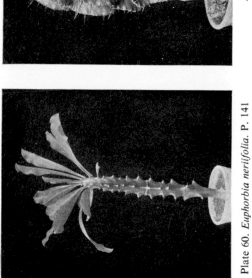

Plate 60. *Euphorbia neriifolia*. P. 141   *Euphorbia polygona*. P. 141

with sharply pointed fleshy leaves, which are flattened on their upper surface and of a greenish-white hue. The flowers are greenish, or greenish-yellow.

Sedum cauticolum. Japan. A lovely species. It has distinct affinities with the well-known *S. Sieboldii,* but differs from this by carrying its leaves in opposite pairs instead of whorls of 3. The rosy-purple flowers appear from September onwards.

Sedum multiceps. Algeria. Has free-branching stems that become brown and woody, the short branches densely furnished with linear fleshy leaves. The flowers, $\frac{1}{2}$ inch in diameter, are bright yellow.

Sedum pulchellum. America. A desirable bright green tufted plant with linear leaves densely arranged on reddish stems. The inflorescence may be up to 4 inches across, and consists of from 3 to 5 recurving branches which radiate from a common centre. One solitary flower grows in this centre, and the rest of the flowers are disposed along the radiating branches. They are bright rosy-purple.

Sedum Morganianum (Plate 52). Popular name "Burro's Tail". An interesting plant, ideal for hanging baskets, producing long stems tightly packed with grey-green leaves. Easily raised from leaf cuttings.

Sedum guatemalense. Looks like a smaller edition of *S. pachyphyllum* but the leaves are deep green and very shiny; if the plant is kept on the dry side, and in the sun, they become a bright cherry-red. An excellent plant for beginners. Easy to propagate from leaves or cuttings.

Sub-Family ECHEVERIOIDEAE

The members of this sub-family are all magnificent plants, both in the form and colour of their leaves and in the richness of their flowers. Botanists have separated several groups of species to form new genera like *Dudleya* and *Urbinia* and these, as well as the genus *Pachyphytum* and the genus *Echeveria*, comprise plants well worth acquiring. A good all-round compost consists of 4 parts loam, 1 part each of sharp sand, broken brick, and old mortar rubble. The growing period is in summer, when water can be freely given; in winter, water every 2 or 3 weeks.

DUDLEYA. The genus is a large one of about 80 species, which are native to the western parts of the United States and Mexico. They have rosettes of white-powdered leaves, but some vary in colour from pale green to grey-green. The flowers are white, pale yellow, yellowish-pink, and red.

Dudleya farinosa (Plate 53). Mexico. Has narrow leaves, $2\frac{1}{2}$ to 3 inches in length, and about $\frac{1}{2}$ inch wide, covered with a white powder. Flowers, greenish-yellow.

Dudleya pulverulenta. S. California. A handsome species. The leaves are spatulate, 6 inches long and about 3 inches broad, the surface heavily powdered as in *D. farinosa*. The red flowers appear in a slender branched raceme, a foot or more in length, furnished with heart-shaped leaves.

URBINIA. A small genus of Mexican plants.

Urbinia agavoides. Forms a compact rosette with a short thick stem. The leaves are about 2 inches in length, very fleshy, pale green with brown tips.

The flowers bright orange, tipped with yellow. There is a monstrous variety, *U. agavoides cristata*.

Urbinia purpusii. Forms a small rosette of dark green leaves marked all over with fine brown spots, with a brown line down the centre of both sides of each leaf. Flowers, carmine.

PACHYPHYTUM. The genus consists of about 9 species. All make handsome and attractive plants by reason of their perfect shape and delicate colouring. All species originate from Mexico. They are easily propagated from cuttings taken in spring and summer.

Pachyphytum bracteosum. The stems may reach a height of about 12 inches, with leaves in loose rosettes with a delicate grey-white bloom. The flower stalk, 12 inches or more in length, carries 10 to 18 bright red flowers.

Pachyphytum oviferum. A most interesting species with whitish-green egg-shaped thick leaves. The flowers are carmine.

ECHEVERIA (Plate 55). The greatest number are natives of Mexico. They form rosettes of varying sizes. Some are low-growing, stemless plants often making clusters. Others form heavy stems with one single large rosette of leaves.

Echeveria carnicolor. Rosettes producing many offsets. The leaves are very fleshy, glaucous, tinted with red. Red flowers, in spikes of 15 to 25, are produced from January to March.

Echeveria Derenbergii (Plate 56). A lovely plant, producing offsets freely. The leaves are spatulate, glaucous, with a red tip, the flowers reddish-yellow.

Echeveria glauca. Has oval leaves reduced to a point at the base, and forming saucer-shaped rosettes. It makes offsets freely. The flower is orange-yellow, with yellow inside. Very easy to grow.

Echeveria gibbiflora. One of the largest species, growing to a height of about 2 feet. The leaves attain a length of about 8 inches and a breadth of about 6 inches; they have a delicate bloom and are frequently of a reddish-brown tint. The flowers are bright red. Var. *metallica* is conspicuous by reason of its pinkish-bronze leaves, with a delicate white or reddish margin. Var. *carunculata* has narrower leaves, but is an interesting variety because of its blister-like growth in the centre of the leaves, which are waxy, almost like translucent alabaster, bluish-white, pinkish, reddish, and pale mauve, all these colours merging into one another. The origin of this plant is not clearly known.

Echeveria leucotricha. A very pretty plant covered with brown felty hairs. The rosettes are 4 to 6 inches in diameter, the leaves very thick. Flowers, red.

Echeveria Peacockii. Forms a compact, regular rosette of long sharply pointed leaves heavily covered with a waxy bloom. Flowers, red, carried on long stalks.

Echeveria pulvinata. A small shrub, bearing rosettes, the leaves loosely set, blunt above, with a short tip. The branches and leaves are covered with soft white hairs.

Echeveria setosa. A small species conspicuous for its neat, soft-haired rosettes, formed of numerous green leaves which are more or less club-shaped, and entirely covered with hairs. Even the bright red, yellow-tipped flowers have white hairs.

Kleinia neriifolia. P. 143

Plate 61. *Kleinia species.* P. 142

Plate 62. *Kleinia tomentosa*. P.143

EUPHORBIACEAE

This very extensive family of plants contains a large number of annual and perennial herbs and woody plants of the ordinary herbaceous type, as well as many plants which are succulents. The most interesting of these are in the genus *Euphorbia*.

EUPHORBIA. These are natives chiefly of S. Africa, where they grow in the deserts or veldt and cover dry mountain slopes, but their distribution is world-wide. The genus contains about 2,000 species. The Euphorbias have a very varied habit and there is an extraordinary similarity of form to the Cactaceae of America, although the two families are quite distinct in their characteristics. Some are thorny, fleshy shrubs, and others have slender branches. Some are columnar with a few or many ribs on the stems and branches, whilst others are spherical, and there are many intermediate forms. Only a few species have leaves, and these leaves are reduced or small, and soon fall off. Some Euphorbias have thorns, and some have none. All have a common characteristic in that they contain a milky juice or latex which is of little merit and often extremely poisonous. A suitable compost is 2 parts loam, 2 parts leaf-mould, 2 parts sharp sand, 2 parts broken brick, and ½ part broken mortar rubble. Cuttings can be rooted in a mixture of fine peat, sand, and charcoal.

Euphorbia bupleurifolia. Cape Province. Has a hard, sometimes almost globular stem like a variety of spherical cactus. Narrow leaves 4 to 5 inches in length grow from its top in spring. The stem will grow to about 4 to 6 inches, with a diameter of about

$3\frac{1}{2}$ inches. The flowers are green to reddish, on short stalks.

Euphorbia caput-medusae. S. Africa. Has a short stem, with numerous grey-green branches, up to 30 inches long, radiating in all directions. The flowers are numerous at the tips of the branches. The species requires full sun and a warm position.

Euphorbia grandidens. S. Africa. A tree-growing species forming several trunks side by side. These give off branches more or less in regular layers, at first erect but later standing out more horizontally, and triangular in section. The edges are somewhat wavy, and provided with pairs of brown thorns.

Euphorbia horrida. S. Africa. Has a low stem, branching at the base, with 12 to 15 or more narrow ribs. There are deep grooves between the ribs, which are notched along the edges.

Euphorbia actea. Indonesia. A vigorous bush, with a straight, erect, 3- or 4-sided trunk 1 to 3 inches in diameter, dark green with a grey marbled band in the centre of almost flat sides; this band curves in feathery fashion towards the edges. Short strong pairs of brown thorns are mounted on hard, round shields.

Euphorbia meloformis (Plate 58). Cape Province. Looks very like a spherical green or grey-green cactus, with 8 to 10 or more ribs regularly marked from the grooves upwards. The growing centre is sunken. Does not require much moisture.

Euphorbia obesa. Cape Province. A much sought after plant. Resembles a small football, varying in size from 3 to 4 inches in diameter, but growing larger with age. The plant body is pale grey-green with rusty coloured, longitudinal and transverse stripes. The growing centre is slightly depressed. This plant should be given all the light possible, especially in winter.

Euphorbia mammillaris (Plate 59). Cape Province. Has more or less cylindrical growths up to 18 inches high, much branched, and covered with 7 to 12 rows of studded ribs. The short-stalked, solitary inflorescences appear in rings around the growing top. The stems do not wither with the flower but remain as long, straight thorns.

Euphorbia neriifolia (Plate 60). E. Indies. Has large leathery leaves, light green and very handsome. It occurs as shrubs and as small trees. The pentagonal stem is highly succulent, and may grow to be very thick. It bears short black thorns. The flowers are almost sessile, small, greenish-yellow to red. There is a cristate form in cultivation.

Euphorbia ingens (Plate 59). Widely distributed from E. Africa to Natal and the Transvaal. It grows into a tree with the trunk branched to form a round head, the branches having 4 thin angles; the thorns are very small or absent.

Euphorbia polygona (Plate 60). In appearance it looks very much like a cactus, growing to a height of 5 or 6 feet, the diameter of the stems being 6 inches or more. The growth is very slow in cultivation and usually the plant remains small. The stems never branch as it forms new growth at the base. Ribs number 10 to 13, and are straight but sometimes twisted, sparsely furnished with ½-inch thorns, which are the remains of the flower stems. The furrows are narrow but deep, almost fissures.

Euphorbia falsa. Very like *E. meloformis*. The flower stems remain after the flowers have withered, giving excellent protection in the wild against animals. The plant makes numerous offsets.

Euphorbia splendens. Madagascar. A very popular plant, with numerous large dark brown branches bearing very sharp thorns. Its popular name is the "Crown of Thorns". The bright green leaves are about 1½ inches long and ¾ inch broad, smooth and leathery. It flowers almost throughout the year, but chiefly in spring, and likes a warm position during the winter. Sometimes listed as *E. Milii*.

Euphorbia valida. Cape Province. Similar to *E. meloformis*. It is spherical when young, but later becomes cylindrical. The old flower stems persist for several years on the plant.

COMPOSITAE

Although this is a very large family of plants, only 3 genera are of interest to growers of succulents. They are *Kleinia*, *Othonna*, and *Senecio*. All require plenty of light and fresh air and during winter a very sparing supply of water, for most species are at rest and moisture at this time of year will easily cause rot. A suitable compost in which to grow these plants is 1 part loam, 2 parts leaf-mould, and 1 part sharp sand.

KLEINIA (Plates 61, 62). Some species are distinguished by bright flowers and white-grey leaves, whilst others are attractive because of their fleshy, glaucous or grey leaves. They are natives of S. Africa, the Canary Islands and Indonesia.

Kleinia acaulis. Cape Province. Has short stems, 2 to 3 inches high, almost cylindrical, pointed, with stalked, greyish-green leaves, about 3 to 6 inches long. The flowers are yellowish.

Plate 63. *Othonna crassifolia* with flowers. P.143

Plate 64. Flower of *Epiphyllum Ackermanii*. P.90
Agave species. P.92

Kleinia articulata. Cape Colony. Its popular name is the "candle plant". The stems are fairly erect, with short joints, varying from 1 to 6 inches in length. These are readily propagated. An easy growing species.

Kleinia gomphophylla. SW. Africa. An interesting plant forming clumps, the branches creeping. The leaves resemble berries, with a spiny tip, and are green with translucent lines. The plant requires a position in full light, with only a moderate amount of water in the growing season.

Kleinia neriifolia (Plate 61). Canary Islands. Has an erect stem and branches of about half an inch in thickness. The grey-green leaves appear in a rosette at the ends of the young stems; they are elliptical, with a short tip.

Kleinia tomentosa (Plate 62). Cape Province. A very lovely plant of white appearance, due to the heavy covering of white felt. Grows up to 12 inches in height. It requires careful attention in winter, but can be frequently watered in the summer growing season.

OTHONNA. The genus consists of about 11 species, native to S. Africa, but only one of these is normally cultivated.

Othonna crassifolia (Plate 63). A useful hanging plant with fleshy leaves of a fresh green colour and bright yellow daisy-like flowers which are produced almost throughout the whole year. The plant is easy to grow, requiring a rich sandy soil, and should be kept fairly moist.

SENECIO. Closely allied to the genus *Kleinia* and native to Cape Province.

Senecio scaposus. Has round fleshy leaves, pencil-shaped, 4 inches long; on the upper surface of the leaves, and just below the tip, a small flattened area occurs. The young leaves are enveloped in a silvery felt-like skin which later breaks open and allows the pale green flesh of the leaves to be seen, giving the older leaves the appearance of being marbled. The flowers are yellow, but of little significance.

Senecio stapeliiformis. As the name implies, the stems of this plant are not unlike, in appearance, the stems of certain Stapelias, but they have 5 to 7 angles furnished with very rough little leaves. Bright red flowers, borne at the end of very long stems, appear in early summer.

BROMELIACEAE

There are many Bromeliads, which grow in very exposed dry places, that have developed tough, leathery leaves, and among them are the Dyckias which are popular with collectors.

DYCKIA. They are mostly natives of Brazil, but a few are to be found in other parts of S. America. Generally speaking, the Dyckias are not difficult subjects for the collector, and do not require much pampering. Most of them enjoy a slightly acid or neutral soil, but they are quite happy in leaf-mould and sand, with a little manure or any good fertilizer added. They enjoy full light conditions and can take plenty of water when the drainage is good. *D. sulphurea*, *D. rariflora*, *D. remotiflora*, *D. coccinea*, *D. minarum*, and *D. simulans* are all small enough to interest the collector limited to pot culture.

All the Dyckias have stiff, spine-edged, succulent leaves. Most of the species have green leaves. The flowers range from sulphur-yellow to orange, and generally appear in spring. They produce offsets which can be easily propagated. Dyckias send out their flower spikes laterally from the side of the plant.

Dyckia sulphurea. Common in most collections. The leaves are bright glossy green above, and striped yellowish-green lengthwise beneath, with hooked teeth along the edges. They form rosettes.

Dyckia rariflora. Not unlike *D. sulphurea*, but the leaves are not as glossy. Along the edges of the leaves, slightly hooked brown-black teeth protrude.

PORTULACACEAE

In this family two genera are found which interest the collector of succulent plants. They are the genus *Anacampseros* and the genus *Portulacaria*.

ANACAMPSEROS. The genus is native to S. Africa. In practically all the species the flowers are rather small. The seed ripens quickly and is dispersed immediately. The genus is divided into four sections: namely, Avonia, Rosulatae, Telephiastrum, and Tuberosae. The Avonia section comprises species of low shrubs. The stems are simple and branched, the roots often tuberous. The leaves are roundish, very small and covered by silvery, scaly, overlapping stipules. The Telephiastrum section comprises low shrubs with stems more or less branching, the leaves often spirally arranged and very fleshy, with long white hairs in the axils. The Rosulatae section and the Tuberosae section contain one species each.

Anacampseros papyracea (Avonia section). Perhaps the best-known species. The stems, 3 to 4 inches in length and more or less prostrate, are covered with dry, papery scales, which are white in the new growth.

Anacampseros ustulata. (Avonia section). Similar to *A. papyracea* but smaller.

Anacampseros Alstonii. (Avonia section). An interesting plant with a root stock turnip-shaped and flat on top. The leaves are covered by silvery, closely adpressed stipules. The flower is whitish.

Great care should be exercised when watering plants in the Avonia section, for all species dislike excess moisture. In winter, they should be kept very dry.

Anacampseros baeseckii (Telephiastrum section). The stems are about 1½ inches high, the leaves growing in a close spiral, pale green with white felt, also covered with bristly hairs, wavy and of a whitish-red. The flower is carmine with a white edge.

Anacampseros rufescens (Telephiastrum section). This species forms clumps with erect stems 2 to 3 inches in height. The thick leaves are greenish on top and reddish underneath, with numerous long bristly hairs. The flower is red.

PORTULACARIA. This genus consists of one species, often found in collections.

Portulacaria afra. S. Africa. A succulent shrub, tree-like, with the fleshy stems branched. The leaves are small, almost round, about ½ inch long. The plants, about 18 inches high, look very like Japanese dwarf trees. Well suited to room cultivation, though it rarely produces flowers, and these are inconspicuous. Propagation is by cuttings, which root easily.

MONTHLY CULTURAL NOTES

JANUARY

Epiphyllums, Zygocacti, Rhipsalis and climbing cacti, the leafy Euphorbias, Crassulas, Echeverias, and Conophytums may be given a very light watering with lukewarm water once or twice during the month if the weather is really fine and sunny.

Ventilate on sunny days and lightly spray your collection of plants, but it is essential that all surplus moisture should have dried away before sundown.

Make plans for the sowing of seeds. Consult the catalogues and decide on the varieties you wish to purchase and grow. Seed-raising is one of the most fascinating phases of the hobby. Keep the temperature of the greenhouse, if the plants are grown there, about 40° to 42°F. during this month.

FEBRUARY

The growing season is approaching and much useful preparatory work can be done this month. Seed and potting composts can be purchased ready mixed, or they can be mixed and got under cover so that, without drying them out, the winter chill has been taken off by the time you wish to use them. Pots and pans can be scrubbed and sterilized.

The greenhouse can be cleaned up. Wipe down the window-panes to admit more light. Check up on your plant labels and names, and it is beneficial to the plants to stir the soil on the surface of the pots, using tweezers or a small fork; this is in order to aerate the soil, and so encourage healthy root growth. Whilst doing this, observe any signs of mealy root aphis attacking the roots, and if any are discovered, set the affected plants aside, later to be cleaned and repotted.

Towards the end of the month, start to sow seeds of succulent plants. Germinate in a temperature of 70° to 80°F.

MARCH

This is a busy month for the enthusiast, for some species of cacti commence new growth. Start to repot any plants requiring it. Sow more seeds.

A little water can be given to the general collection about once a week. Avoid splashing water over the plants, for if it remains on the plants overnight there is a risk of rot setting in, but a light spraying early in the day when the weather is fine will do no harm.

As light is an important factor to the growth of plants, keep the greenhouse glass clean in order to admit all the light possible. Your plants are still tender from the lack of light and sun during the winter, and some shade may be required in really bright sunshine, but as plants become used to more light, the temporary shading can be dispensed with.

APRIL

Continue to repot plants. After repotting, do not water them again for a few days. It is usual to repot small plants annually and larger ones every two or three years. This month tall-stemmed Echeverias can be beheaded and rooted afresh to make neat short-stemmed plants. Dry the tops after cutting them off for a week or longer, to ensure a good callus. Root the tops in dry sand or vermiculite.

At the beginning of the month, withhold further supplies of water from Conophytums. These should now remain dry until August.

MAY

The majority of succulent plants should now be growing well, and many varieties will be in flower.

Watering may be done once a week. The frequency, however, depends on weather conditions, and to a large extent upon your soil, as some soils retain moisture longer than others. When watering, water well and allow the soil to dry out before watering again.

Towards the end of the month, Lithops may receive their first watering of the year, provided most of last year's leaf pair has dried away, but water should be sparingly given at first.

By the end of the month give plenty of fresh air to the plants when the weather is favourable, but avoid draughts.

Keep a sharp look-out for pests which may now become active, particularly the mealy bug and red spider (see section on Pest Control).

Continue with the sowing of seeds.

This is a good time to take cuttings. Sometimes an old plant which looks unhealthy can have its healthy parts cut off and these treated as cuttings (see section on Propagation).

JUNE

Your plants can now be watered once or twice a week, and an occasional light spraying will be beneficial, but avoid flower buds or flowers, for water may cause damage to them. Air should be admitted freely.

Throughout this month, and until the end of August, continue to take cuttings. Besides Conophytums, Pleiospilos should also be kept dry until the end of July. Succulent plants are sun-lovers, but there are a few that prefer light shade. Of these, Epiphyllums, Rhipsalis, Ceropegias, Gasterias, and Haworthias will respond better in shade than if grown in full light.

Epiphyllums should now be in bloom. Cuttings of these can be taken this month.

This is an ideal month for grafting. Many species of succulent plants like to grow out of doors in summer. Choose the sunniest part of the garden and sink the plants in their pots into the soil, or, if this is not possible, place the plants in any sunny spot out-of-doors.

JULY

Echeverias, Pachyphytums, Sedums and Crassulas propagate easily this month from leaf cuttings (see section on Propagation). *Euphorbia* cuttings can be rooted. When these are selected they should be taken at a junction of a branch or section with the main stem. They are apt to be slow to propagate, partly because of the abundant latex that exudes from the cut surface. Sometimes, if the cutting is given a quick dip into water, this will remove the latex and stop the flow. Dry the cuttings thoroughly for two or three weeks before placing in the rooting material. Bottom heat is helpful to quick rooting, and the cutting should not be buried but should rest on the surface of the compost, held in position by a small cane.

Epiphyllums should now be given a period of rest for a month or so. This is a good time to repot those plants requiring it. Usually the new shoots appear in late summer. The plants will benefit greatly if, for the next few weeks, they can be placed out-of-doors in some shade.

Start to water Conophytums and Pleiospilos. Anyone going on holiday this month need not worry about leaving their plants providing they plunge them, pot and all, out-of-doors in the garden, and give them a good soaking before leaving home.

SEPTEMBER

Succulent plants which flowered early in the season such as *Echinopsis* and some of the *Cereus*, should be repotted early in September rather than in the spring, otherwise flower buds are apt to dry off. After repotting do not water again for a few days in case of rot setting in, following possible damage to the roots. Many plants continue to make strong growth and, although we are still having sunny days, the nights are getting longer and cooler. Great care should therefore once more be exercised when watering. If the weather is dull and cool, reduce the watering to about once a week. Avoid evening watering. Soon the plants will be resting, and it is necessary now to start preparing them for the winter's rest. There are certain exceptions, however. Stapelias flower well this month and still require fair amounts of water. Kleinias, Senecios, and Crassulas are at their best and need reasonable amounts, as do Lithops and Conophytums.

At the end of the month, bring any plants you may have had in the garden, or outside the window, back to the window-sill or the greenhouse.

OCTOBER

Watering must now be reduced, but such plants as Epiphyllums, Rhipsalis, Kleinias, and Conophytums should continue to have a reasonably moist soil. If heating apparatus is used in the greenhouse, this should be checked over, for soon you may want to use it. Keep a sharp look-out for sudden early frosts. A double layer of newspaper round or over your plants will give some protection if a sudden fall in temperature is expected and you have no heating. When the curtains are drawn, plants growing on a window-sill should be protected from frost and draughts by bringing them into the room. They should never be left between the curtain and the window-frame as on cold nights there is always the risk of frost near the window.

NOVEMBER

On really sunny days, you can still give a little water to plants where the soil has dried up unduly, but great care is necessary not to overdo it.

DECEMBER

Epiphyllums, Zygocacti, Rhipsalis, Echeverias, Crassulas, Kleinias, Senecios, Haworthias, Aeoniums, Euphorbias, Conophytums, can have an occasional light watering to prevent them shrivelling. Endeavour during the month to keep the air, especially in the greenhouse, as dry as possible. High temperatures are unnecessary, for the plants will winter safely at 40° to 42°F.

Zygocactus plants will be showing buds, and a fortnightly feed with a liquid plant food will be beneficial to them. As the buds are very delicate and are drawn towards the light, every care should be exercised to see that the plants are not turned, but remain always in the same position, otherwise the buds may drop off.

GLOSSARY

ACUTE: ending in a point less than a right angle.

ADVENTITIOUS BUDS: buds appearing in unusual places.

ALTERNATE: applied to leaves placed at different heights up the stem.

ANTHER: the pollen-bearing part of a stamen, usually divided into two cells or pouches.

AREOLE: area or centre of growth.

AWL-SHAPED: sharp-pointed from a broader base.

CACTACEAE: the botanical name for cacti.

CAESPITOSE: growing in close tufts.

CENTRAL SPINES: the inner spines of a spine cluster.

COMPRESSED: flattened on opposite sides.

CRENULATE: finely notched or scalloped.

CYME: a branched inflorescence where the central flower opens first.

EPIDERMIS: the outermost layer or cells of the leaf, etc.

FILAMENT: the stalk part of a stamen which supports the anther.

FISSURE: a furrow caused by splitting.

GIBBOUS: convex, rounded, protuberant.

GLABROUS: smooth, free from hair.

GLAUCOUS: pale bluish-green or whitish-green.

GLOBOSE: ball-like, nearly spherical.

GLOCHID: barbed hair.

HABITAT: the locality where the plant is found.

INFLORESCENCE: the mass of the flowers and their pedicels grouped around the principal branch.

KEEL: the central dorsal ridge.

LANCEOLATE: lance-shaped.

LINEAR: long and narrow with parallel margins.

LOBE: a more or less deep division of floral organs or leaves.

OBOVATE: in the shape of an egg, point downwards.

OBTUSE: blunt or rounded at the tip.

PAPILLAE: small, rounded elevations of the epidermis.

PAPILLOSE: covered with papillae.

PEDICEL: the last division of a divided peduncle which bears the flower.

PEDUNCLE: axis or stalk bearing flowers, often branched.

PERIANTH: the coloured floral envelope representing the petals and sepals.

RACEME: a simple inflorescence of pedicelled flowers scattered along an unbranched common axis.

RADIAL SPINES: the outer spines of a cluster.

RECURVING: curving backwards or downwards.

SEPALS: the outer circle of flower leaves, green or coloured.

SESSILE: without a stalk.

SHRUB: a woody plant branching from the base.

SPATULATE: shaped like a spatula with the tip broadened and rounded.

SPINE: a hardened and sharply pointed modified branch or leaf, called also a thorn.

STAMEN: the male pollen-bearing organ consisting of anther and filament.

STIGMA: the tip of the style on which the pollen is deposited.

STIPULE: small, leaf-like appendage to a leaf, usually at the base of the leaf-stem.

STOMATA: the minute pores in the epidermis of a leaf communicating with internal air cavities.

STYLE: the stalk joining the ovary and the stigma.

SUCCULENT: juicy, fleshy.

TOMENTOSE: densely hairy with short hairs.

TRANSLUCENT: partially transparent.

TUBERCLES: knobby projections

UMBEL: an inflorescence with the flower stalks radiating from the stem like the ribs of an umbrella.

WHORLS: arrangement of plant parts in a circle around the stem.

INDEX

PRINTED FOR THE PUBLISHERS
BY JARROLD AND SONS LTD, NORWICH
762-360